COLLECTOR'S GUIDE TO
P.EZ ®
IDENTIFICATION & PRICE GUIDE
2nd Edition

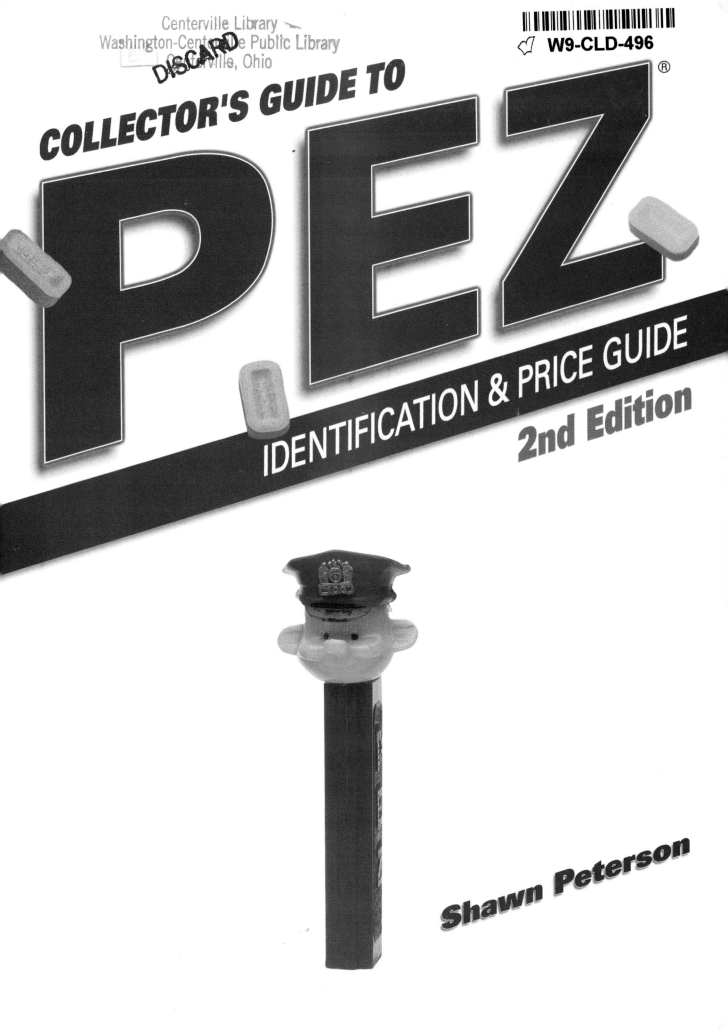

Shawn Peterson

Published by

kp **krause publications**
An F&W Publications Company

700 East State Street • Iola, WI 54990-0001
715-445-2214 • 888-457-2873
www.krause.com

Please call or write for our free catalog of antiques and collectibles publications.
To place an order or receive our free catalog, call (800) 258-0929 or, use our regular business telephone
(715) 445-2214.

Library of Congress Catalog Number: 00-110082
ISBN: 0-87349-540-3
Printed in the United States of America

CONTENTS

ACKNOWLEDGMENTS

A special thank you to:

My parents, John and Lorrene for their continued support and help at all of those St. Louis conventions!

Maryanne and Paul Kennedy who first gave this book project of mine "legs" when they allowed me to turn their living room into a photo studio back on that fall day in 2000, Thank You! Maryanne is truly one of the most knowledgeable, friendly collectors around and has one of the most impressive PEZ collections ever assembled.

Johann Patek who was kind enough to share his time, knowledge, and collection with me. Johann is one of Europe's leading collectors and has some of the rarest PEZ items known to exist. Not only is Johann an expert PEZ collector, he served as our tour guide, chauffeur, translator, banker, and at one point—the cook! Thanks Johann, it was a trip I will never forget!

Krause Publications, my project manager Karen O'Brien, Paul Kennedy in acquisitions, Kevin Sauter for his cover design, Donna Mummery for the book's interior graphic design, and everyone who worked on this project, thank you!

Thanks to the following people for their help, contributions, and friendship: Steve Warner (photography), Richard Belyski, Dora Dwyer, Gerhard Trebbin and Silvia Biermayr, the PEZ company, Adam Young, Nick Petracca, John LaSpina, and Gerda Jahn.

Unless otherwise noted, all photos are from the author's personal collection.

PEZ® is used throughout this book as a registered trademark. This book is neither a product of or endorsed by PEZ® Candy Inc.

ABOUT THE AUTHOR

Shawn Peterson started collecting PEZ® in 1990 while going to weekend flea markets. At that time he didn't really collect much of anything and just went for something to do. After noticing several tables with small boxes full of PEZ® dispensers he decided to buy some to take home. After all, they were just .50 cents apiece and "I couldn't leave without buying something!" His collection started with about a dozen dispensers, nothing special just common variety footed dispensers, but it slowly started to grow. The next year the very first picture book showing all the known dispensers appeared and that was it. "After seeing that book I was hooked, I was on a mission to find PEZ® dispensers! I had no idea that there were so many different ones." What started as a whim quickly grew into an obsession that now takes up much of his free time. "I wouldn't trade it for anything, I've been places and met people from all over the world that I ordinarily wouldn't have. PEZ® collectors are great. It's really been a lot of fun!"

When he is not roaming the country with his job at Hallmark Cards or attending a PEZ® convention you can find him at home in the Kansas City area. In addition to PEZ® dispensers Shawn also collects KISS memorabilia and "anything else I just can't do without." He has had his collection on public display at Crown Center and the Toy and Miniature Museum Kansas City as well as featured in *Toy Shop* magazine. Shawn is always interested in adding to his collection. You may contact him at: P.O. Box 571, Blue Springs, MO 64013-0571

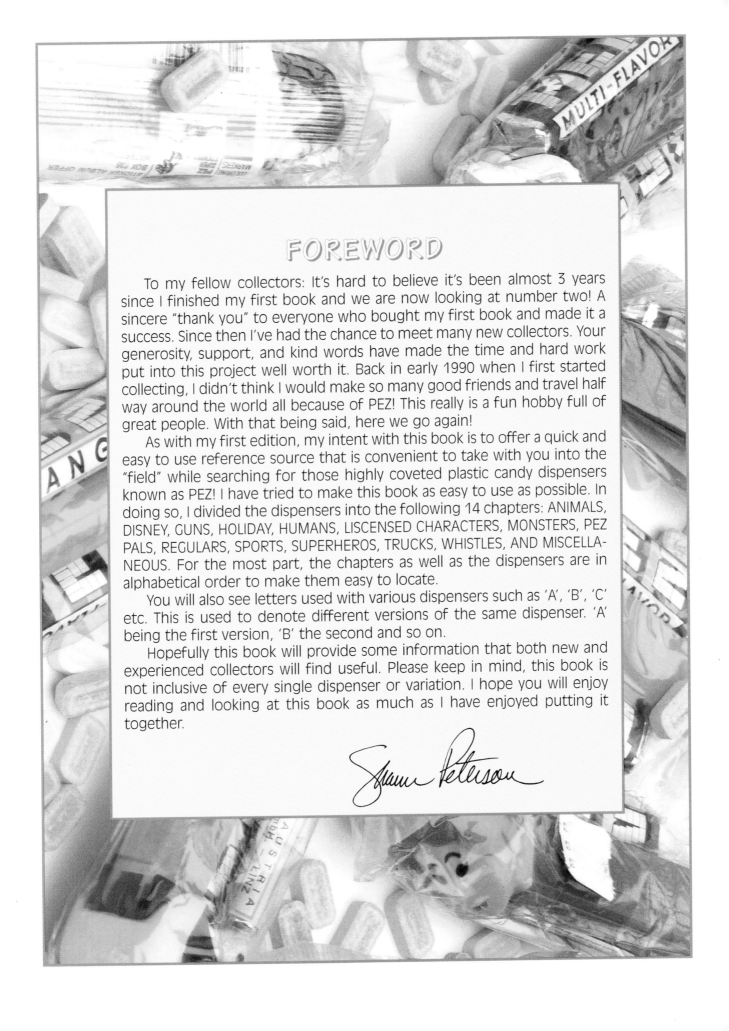

FOREWORD

To my fellow collectors: It's hard to believe it's been almost 3 years since I finished my first book and we are now looking at number two! A sincere "thank you" to everyone who bought my first book and made it a success. Since then I've had the chance to meet many new collectors. Your generosity, support, and kind words have made the time and hard work put into this project well worth it. Back in early 1990 when I first started collecting, I didn't think I would make so many good friends and travel half way around the world all because of PEZ! This really is a fun hobby full of great people. With that being said, here we go again!

As with my first edition, my intent with this book is to offer a quick and easy to use reference source that is convenient to take with you into the "field" while searching for those highly coveted plastic candy dispensers known as PEZ! I have tried to make this book as easy to use as possible. In doing so, I divided the dispensers into the following 14 chapters: ANIMALS, DISNEY, GUNS, HOLIDAY, HUMANS, LISCENSED CHARACTERS, MONSTERS, PEZ PALS, REGULARS, SPORTS, SUPERHEROS, TRUCKS, WHISTLES, AND MISCELLA-NEOUS. For the most part, the chapters as well as the dispensers are in alphabetical order to make them easy to locate.

You will also see letters used with various dispensers such as 'A', 'B', 'C' etc. This is used to denote different versions of the same dispenser. 'A' being the first version, 'B' the second and so on.

Hopefully this book will provide some information that both new and experienced collectors will find useful. Please keep in mind, this book is not inclusive of every single dispenser or variation. I hope you will enjoy reading and looking at this book as much as I have enjoyed putting it together.

Shawn Peterson

CHAPTER 1

PEZ History

The PEZ® dispenser has been around for 50 years. PEZ® candy got its start even earlier, introduced in 1927 in Vienna, Austria as the world's first-ever breath mint. Edward Haas, an avid non-smoker, wanted to invent a product to rival cigarettes. His product, a small compressed sugar tablet with peppermint oil added, was sold in small pocket size tins (similar to Altoid brand mints of today) and marketed as an alternative to smoking. His slogan was "smoking prohibited-pezzing allowed!" But what is "pezzing," or better yet, PEZ®? The name "Pez" was derived from the German word for peppermint, "pfefferminz." Using the first, middle, and last letter of the word, Haas came up with the name "Pez." Twenty years after the candy was invented, in 1948, Oscar Uxa invented and patented a little mechanical box for dispensing the candy. Resembling a Bic cigarette lighter, the dispenser was marketed as an upscale adult product. The PEZ® "box" had moderate success in Europe, and in 1952 Haas decided to try and conquer the U.S. market. In the span of less than 2 years, he realized that PEZ® was not going to be a worthwhile venture in the United States.

Haas did not give up however, and he decided to reinvent the product by adding fruit flavors to the candy—and a three-dimensional cartoon head to the top of the dispenser. What a success this turned out to be, combining two of kids' favorite things: candy and a toy! This marketing shift proved to be a brilliant move, making PEZ® one of the most recognizable commercial names around. It is hard to say how many different heads have graced the top of a PEZ® dispenser. Different versions of the same character have been produced and, in some cases, the same version has come in multiple color variations. Conservative estimates put the number between 250-300 different heads.

Despite numerous requests for Elvis and others, PEZ® has never depicted a real person with the exception of Betsy Ross, Paul Revere, and Daniel Boone. They have followed this policy for two main reasons: real people rarely have interestingly shaped heads, and, secondly, the possibility of a real person winding up in a front-page controversy makes the thought less than appealing for a children's product. The company also tries to stay away from passing fads, using only characters that have stood the test of time. At any given time there are as many as 60-70 different dispensers available at local retailers, not to mention the seasonal ones that appear for such holidays as Christmas, Easter, Halloween, and Valentines Day. PEZ® began offering limited edition dispensers in 1998 with remakes of the classic psychedelic hand and flower. Offered only through the PEZ® Candy Inc. via phone or their Web site, these limited editions have proven quite popular with collectors.

PEZ®, the company, is divided into two separate entities, PEZ® USA and PEZ® International. PEZ® USA, located in Orange, Connecticut, is responsible for North American distribution, packaging dispensers, and making candy. PEZ® International, now located in Traun, Austria, handles distribution for the rest of the world, along with packaging dispensers and making candy. Although they are separately managed companies, they communicate with each other and sometimes share the cost of producing a new dispenser. The fact that they are two separate companies accounts for the reason some dispensers commonly found in the United States are not found anywhere else in the world and vise versa. Depending on how you look at it, this can make collecting more fun or more of a challenge. PEZ® USA is a privately owned business and will not release sales figures to the public, but they do insist that they sell more dispensers per year than there are kids in the United States. Their staff works in three

PEZ® factory in Orange, Connecticut.

shifts, 24 hours a day, producing the candy and packaging dispensers for shipment all across North America.

The dispenser itself has seen a few modest changes over the years. One of the biggest changes happened in the late 1980s when "feet" where added to the bottom of the dispenser base to give it more stability when standing upright. Numerous candy and fruit flavors have been produced, ranging from apple to chocolate. Some flavors were more popular than others, and some were just plain strange like chlorophyll, flower, and eucalyptus. Currently the flavors available in the United States are lemon, orange, grape, strawberry, peppermint and the four new sour flavors: green apple, watermelon, pineapple, and blue raspberry.

Although PEZ® has a long history, only recently has it become a hot collectible. PEZ® collecting has been gathering steam since the early 1990s when the first guidebook appeared, depicting all known dispensers and their rarity. The first ever PEZ® convention was held in Mentor, Ohio on Saturday, June 15th 1991. Several other conventions around the country soon followed. Collectors finally had a chance to meet each other, buy and sell PEZ®, and view rare and unusual dispensers on display. Conventions have quickly become must-attend events for addicted collectors, drawing people from all over the United States and even all over the world.

In 1993, the prestigious Christie's auction house in New York took notice of this evolving hobby and held it's first ever pop culture auction featuring PEZ®. The auction realized record prices, taking the hobby to a new level. PEZ® has been featured in countless magazines, TV shows, and news articles—landing on the cover of *Forbes* magazine in December of 1993. The popular Seinfeld television show even had an episode featuring a Tweety Bird PEZ® dispenser. All this notoriety hasn't gone unnoticed. More and more people have begun to collect these cute character pieces,

sending prices into the hundreds and even thousands of dollars for a single dispenser.

PEZ® has done very little in the way of advertising, relying on impulse purchases and parents buying for their kids on a nostalgic whim. While this may not seem like the best marketing method, the company claims it can barely keep up with demand. PEZ® has even become a very popular licensee, with companies vying to put the PEZ® name on everything from clocks to coffee mugs. Hallmark has featured these collectibles on a puzzle and matching greeting card, and has also produced two different PEZ® dispenser Christmas ornaments.

No one can say for sure where this hobby will go, or if the dispensers will continue to hold their value. In the years that I have been a collector, prices, as well as the collector base, have steadily grown. At present, this hobby has two things in it's favor; demand far surpasses the supply of vintage dispensers, and PEZ® is still produced today and can be found in almost any grocery or discount store, making it available to a whole new generation of collectors. With new additions added regularly, the continued success of PEZ® is almost certainly assured.

Silver glow from the early '90s

PEZ® factory in Traun, Austria.

CHAPTER 2

Pricing Information

A price guide should be viewed as just that – a guide. Since this hobby has become organized, PEZ® prices, like the stock market, have been in nearly constant motion. Prices not only go up, but some DO go down. Several factors account for this fluctuation: supply and demand, emotion, and quantity finds. To pick a point in time and label a dispenser worth exactly "X" amount of dollars, in my opinion, is not in the best interest of the collector. I feel that an average price system is more useful. I have used several sources – on-line auctions, dealer's lists, and other collectors – to determine what I feel is an accurate price range for each dispenser. Therefore, a price quoted will not reflect the top or bottom dollar that a dispenser has sold for. Dispensers that do not appear for sale often enough to determine an accurate price range will be represented with a price and the "+" symbol.

This pricing information should be used for dispensers that are complete and void of any missing pieces, cracks, chips, or melt marks, and have working spring mechanisms. Dispensers that are broken or missing pieces are not worth nearly as much as complete dispensers. Pricing incomplete or broken dispensers is very subjective. Missing pieces are almost never found. Some collectors don't mind if a dispenser is broken or missing a piece or two, especially if it is a rare dispenser or variation. They may be happy just to have an example in their collection, and hope to upgrade to a dispenser in better condition.

Generally, the value of a dispenser is in the head. Age, country of origin, stem, and patent numbers can also play a part, but are commonly thought of as non-determining factors when assessing the value. Exceptions to this regarding the stems are features such as die-cuts, advertising, or pictures, such as the one found on the witch regular. One or more of these features can actually increase the value of the dispenser. Other stem characteristics must be present in certain dispensers to complete the value and be considered correct. For example, the football player stem will have one smooth side with an upside down pennant-shaped triangle molded in. Also, all of the original psychedelics will have at least one, and sometimes two, smooth sides to which a sticker was applied (stickers must still be intact). Swirled or marbleized stems can also add value to a dispenser. Some collectors are willing to pay a bit more for these as they can be very difficult to find and no two are exactly alike. Finally, resale is something you may want to consider. A complete, mint condition dispenser will always be easier to sell than one that has problems or is missing parts.

A Word of Caution

Collectors beware: some people have begun making and selling reproduction parts for PEZ®. Some are better skilled at this than others. Trust your instinct. If you think an item is questionable, it is better to pass than find out later that you have been fooled. Know what you are buying and be familiar with how a piece should look.

Some dispensers, such as Elvis and Kiss, were never made by PEZ® but can be found with relative ease. How can this be? When a dispenser of a certain character or person is in demand but does not exist, collectors have sometimes resorted to making their own dispensers. These are known as "fan-made" or "fantasy" pieces. Again, some of these pieces are better made than others; in fact some are quite good. You can even find fantasy pieces that are mint on a very convincing PEZ® card, but in reality never existed. Most of these dispensers sell in the $25 or less range and are considered by some to be very collectable.

Only knowledge, experience, and buying from a well known, reputable dealer will help avoid having a reproduction or fake unknowingly passed on to you. Common reproduction parts include but are not limited to: the ringmaster's mustache, the Mexican's goatee and earrings, the policeman's and fireman's hat badges, the knight's plume, the doctor's reflector, and Batman's cape. Most parts are not labeled as reproductions. For instance, a remake of the doctor's reflector is made of aluminum instead of plastic, and the reproduction capes for Batman are usually much thicker than the vintage capes. Studying pictures in books and going to PEZ® conventions are your best sources for comparing dispensers. A great deal of information can also be found on the Internet. There are many PEZ® related Web sites made by collectors that will answer almost any question related to the hobby.

How to Use this Guide

The dispensers are listed in the first portion of the book, divided into subject categories. The common name of the dispenser is listed first, followed by any alternate names. Next you will find a date—this is when production of the dispenser started. Notes on whether the dispenser was made with or without feet (or both) are also included. Finally, a value will be given for the dispenser as well as for known variations.

Values given are for loose dispensers complete with all working parts, and have no melt marks, cracks or chips. Pricing packaged dispensers is a bit more subjective. Some collectors have little or no interest in packaged dispensers, as they want to display their collections more creatively. Currently, there is little interest in poly bag packaging. Clear cello bags may add a little value to a dispenser. For example, if the dispenser is worth $50, it might bring $55-$60 if packaged in a clear cello bag. The exceptions to this are dispensers that are packaged with an insert, sticker, comic, advertising, or a rare pack of candy. Sometimes these inserts are worth more than the dispenser. Dispensers mounted on cards are considered the most desirable of packaged dispensers. Factors affecting the value of a carded dispenser are condition of the card, and graphics or artwork on the card. Seasonal cards with neat artwork are worth more than plain, solid color cards.

CHAPTER 3

Animals

Bugz! Released summer of 2000. (L to R) Beetle, Grasshopper, Butterfly, Fly, and Bee.

Sweet Ladybird, Crystal Sweet Ladybird, Clumsy Worm, Crystal Clumsy Worm.

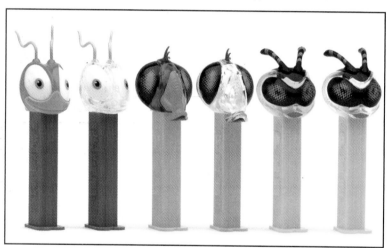

Crystal Bugz Set - Flutterfly, Fly, Bee.

Bugz

Summer, 2000 With Feet
The PEZ® Web site calls them (L to R) Barney Beetle, Jumpin' Jack the grasshopper, Florence Flutterfly, Sam Snuffle the fly, Super Bee, Sweet Ladybird the lady bug, the clumsy worm, and good natured centipede.

Value: $1-$2 each
Crystal Bugz: $4-$6 each

Caterpillar

Caterpillar, Crystal Caterpillar, Beetle, Grasshopper, Crystal Grasshopper.

The "smart bee" or baby bee.

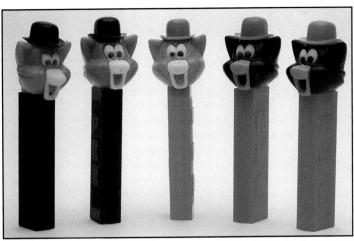

Cat with Derby

(also known as Puzzy Cat)

Early 1970s, No Feet
Several head and hat color combinations are available, as are many stem colors. The blue hat version is the rarest, selling for twice that of other versions.

Value:	$85-$95
Blue Hat:	$150-$175

Cockatoo

Mid-1970s, No Feet and With Feet
Several head and beak color combinations are available. The peach-colored beak is harder to find and worth slightly more than other colors.

No Feet:	$65-$85
With Feet:	$45-$65

Cow A

Early 1970s, No Feet
There are many different color variations of the head. The green head is a rare variation and sells for two to three times as much as other versions.

Value:	$100-$125

Several color variations of the Cockatoo dispenser.

Cow B

Mid-1970s, No Feet
Many different color combinations can be found. The same mold was used to make the head for the Yappy Dog.

Value:	$85-$120

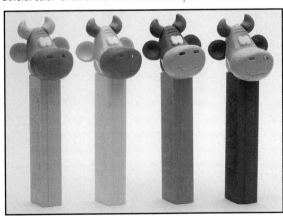

Many color combinations can be found of the Cow B dispenser. (Green and yellow cow from the Maryann Kennedy collection)

Brown cow "A" variation. (From the Johann Patek collection)

Cow A. The green-head version on the far left is a rare variation. (Green head cow from the Maryann Kennedy collection)

Crazy Animals (L to R): Frog, Shark, Octopus, and Camel.

Crazy Animals

Released fall 1999, With Feet
Not sold in the U.S.
Four Animals: Frog, Shark, Octopus, and Camel

Value: $1-$3

Crocodile

Mid-1970s, No Feet
Can be found in several shades of green and even in purple. The purple version sells for about twice as much as green dispensers.

**Value
(green head crocodiles):**
$100-$125

Crocodile from the mid-1970s.

Crystal Dinosaurs. This series was only available through a PEZ® mail-in offer.

Crystal Dinosaur

1999, With Feet
Only available through PEZ® mail-in offer.

Value: $3-$5

Duck with Flower. Many color combinations can be found of this dispenser.

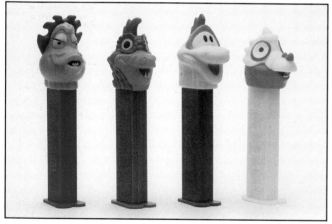

Dinosaurs. (L to R): She-Saur, Fly-Saur, He-Saur, and I-Saur.

Dinosaurs

Early 1990s, With Feet
The dinosaurs were first released in Europe in the early 1990s and were known as the "Trias Family"—Brutus, Titus, Chaos, and Venesia. Shortly thereafter, they were introduced to the United States as "Pez-a-Saurs."

Value: $1-$2

Duck with Flower

Early 1970s, No Feet
Many head, flower, and beak color combinations can be found. Black, Orange, and Yellow are the hardest head colors to find and usually sell for twice as much as other color variations.

Value:	$80-$100
Yellow Head:	$125-$150
Black or Orange Head:	$175-$200

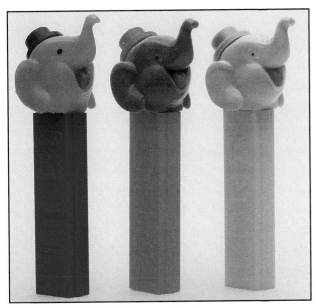

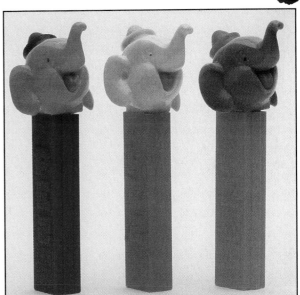

Elephant with Flat Hat.
(Pink elephant from the Maryann Kennedy collection)

Elephant with Pointy Hat.

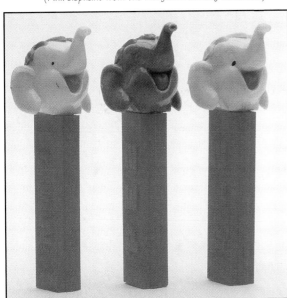

Elephant (also known as Circus Elephant or Big Top Elephant)

Early 1970s, No Feet

There are three different variations to the elephant regarding its head gear—flat hat, pointy hat, and hair. The elephant came in many different color combinations, some of which, such as the pink head variation, are tough to find.

Flat hat:	**$100-$125**
Pointy hat:	**$125-$150**
Hair:	**$150-$175**

Elephant with Hair.

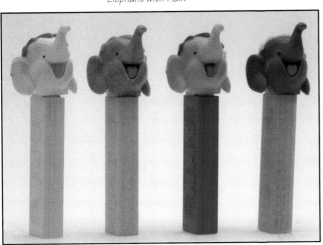

Some variations of elephants with hair.
(From the Johann Patek collection)

Some variations of elephants with flat hats.
(From the Johann Patek collection)

Giraffe

Mid-1970s, No Feet
This is one of the tougher animal dispensers to find.
Value: $175-$200

Two examples of the Gorilla.

Giraffe from the mid-1970s.

Gorilla

Mid-1970s, No Feet
This dispenser was produced with a black, brown or orange head.
Value: $80-$95

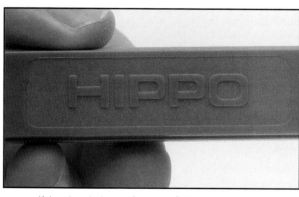

Unique inscription on the stem of the Hippo dispenser.
(From the Maryann Kennedy collection)

The Hippo was not released in the U.S. and is very difficult to find.
(From the Maryann Kennedy collection)

Right side of the Hippo dispenser.

Hippo

Early 1970s, No Feet
Among the rarest of the animal dispensers, the hippo was not released in the United States and is very difficult to find. The Hippo is unusual in that it has an entire body on top of the stem rather than just a head.
Value: $900-$1000

"Misfit" elephant and lion (also known as the David W. lion) were only available through a mail-in offer.

Kooky Zoo Characters. (L to R): Blinky Bill, Lion, Gator, Hippo, and Elephant.

Colored crystal Kooky Zoo characters.

Kooky Zoo Series

Late 1990s, With Feet

Series includes Blinky Bill, a koala and licensed Australian comic character, Lion, Gator, Hippo, and Elephant. A crystal series was available in 1999 through a PEZ® mail-in offer.

A pink elephant and a lion were also released by PEZ® Candy Inc. as part of their "misfits" mail-in offer.

Value:	**$2-$6 each**
Crystal Series:	**$3-$5 each**
Misfit Elephant and Lion:	**$3-$5 each**
Zinnafant Elephant:	**$25-$30**

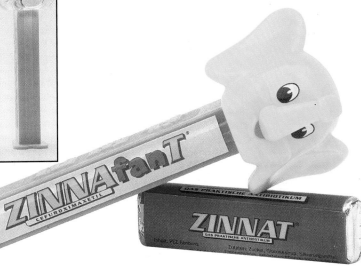

Kooky Zoo Crystal Series (L to R): Hippo, Elephant, Lion, and Gator.

"Zinnafant" elephant. Done by a European drug company to promote a new antibiotic drug called "Zinnat." Should come with matching candy pack to be considered complete.

15

Lil Lion

Late 1960s, No Feet
Value: $70-$90

The friendly looking Lil Lion from the late 1960s.

Variations of the Lion with Crown. The very tough to find red face with white crown goes for twice the price of other variations. (From the Maryann Kennedy collection)

Lion with Crown

Mid-1970s, No Feet
This dispenser can be found with several subtle green face color variations and many other different color combinations. The very tough to find red face with white crown goes for twice the price of other variations. Some rare variations can sell for more than double the price.
Value: $125-$175
Red Face/White Crown: $200-$250

Hard to find Lion with Crown variations. (From the Johann Patek collection)

Lion's Club dispenser with
PEZ® side of stem showing.

Lion's Club dispenser with
Lion's Club inscription.

Lions Club

1962, No Feet
A unique, interesting, and hard to find dispenser. Consul Haas was the president of Lions Club, Austria. He commissioned the dispenser for the purpose of handing them out to members who attended the 1962 International Lions Club convention in Nice, France. After the convention, the few pieces of remaining stock had the inscribed stem removed and replaced with a generic PEZ® stem. It was sold in the Circus assortment.

Inscribed stem: **$3000+**
Generic stem: **$2000+**

A red head variation of the Lions Club dispenser with generic stem. (From the Johann Patek collection)

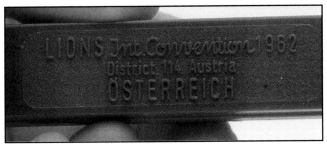

Stem inscription reads: Lions Int. Convention 1962, District 114 Austria, Österreich. (Lions Club dispenser from the Maryann Kennedy collection)

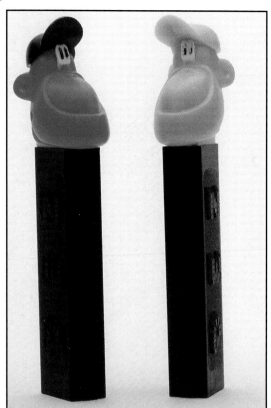

Mimic the Monkey is also known as "Monkey with Ball Cap."

Mimic the Monkey

(Also known as Monkey with Ball Cap)

Mid-1970s, No Feet and With Feet
Many different head colors were produced, making this an especially fun dispenser to try and collect all variations. Head colors include orange, yellow, red, and blue.

No Feet: $45-$60
With Feet: $40-$50

Monkey Sailor from the late 1960s. The same dispenser, with a "J" added to the cap, was used as a Donkey Kong Jr. dispenser in the 1980s.

Monkey Sailor

Late 1960s, No Feet
The same dispenser was used as Donkey Kong Jr. with one exception, a small transparent sticker was added on his cap with the letter "J." The Donkey Kong Jr. was a 1984 Ralston Purina cereal premium.

Monkey Sailor: $60-$80
Donkey Kong Jr. with box: $400-$500

Octopus

Early 1970s, No Feet
The Octopus can be found in red, orange or black.

Orange: $85-$95
Black: $90-$120
Red: $125-$150

Two examples of the Octopus.

Panda (L to R): Current version, Stencil Eyes-No Feet, and Removable eyes.

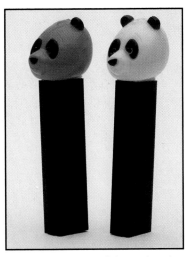

Two rare variations of the panda—the yellow and red heads. (From the Maryann Kennedy collection)

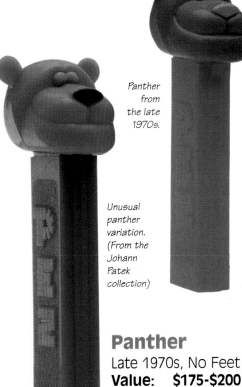

Panther from the late 1970s.

Unusual panther variation. (From the Johann Patek collection)

Panda
Early 1970s, No Feet and With Feet
The Panda has undergone a few modest changes but can still be found today. Rare and hard to find colors include the yellow and red head versions.

Removable eyes version (oldest):	$25-$35
Yellow or Red head (with removable eyes):	$300+
No Feet, stencil eyes:	$10-$20
Current version:	$1-$2

Panther
Late 1970s, No Feet
Value: **$175-$200**

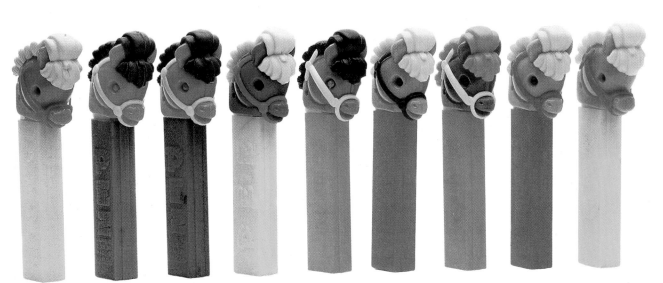

The Pony, also known as the Pony-Go-Round, can be found in many different colors. The green, pink, and purple heads are less common variations and can bring up to five times as much as more common color variations. (Green, pink, and purple-head ponies from the Maryann Kennedy collection)

Pony (also known as Pony-Go-Round)
Early 1970s, No Feet
This dispenser can be found in MANY different colors and it's fun to search for variations. Some are very difficult to find such as the green, pink, and purple heads and these versions can bring up to five times as much as the more common color combinations.
Value (common color combinations):   **$100-$150**

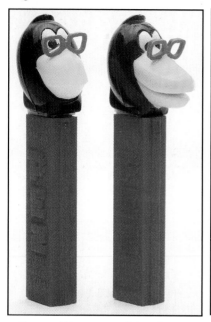

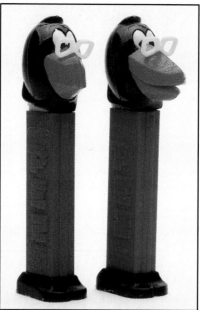

Short and long versions of the yellow-beak Raven. (Long beak from the Maryann Kennedy collection)

Short and long versions of the red-beak Raven. (Long beak from the Maryann Kennedy collection)

Raven

Early 1970s, No Feet and With Feet
Two versions were made of the Raven—one with a short beak and one with a long beak. The beak can be found in either yellow or red. The long beak was not released in the U.S. and usually sells for about twice that of the regular version.

Short Beak, No Feet:	**$75-$90**
Short Beak, Feet:	**$50-$75**
Long Beak:	**$150-$200**

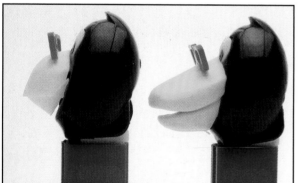

Side-view comparison of the short and long-beak versions of the Raven. (Long beak from the Maryann Kennedy collection)

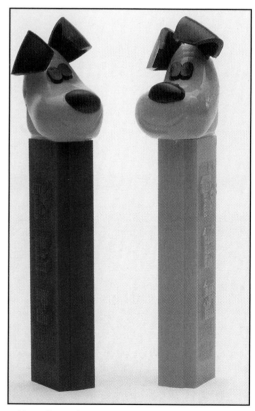

Yappy Dog—this same head was also used on Cow B.

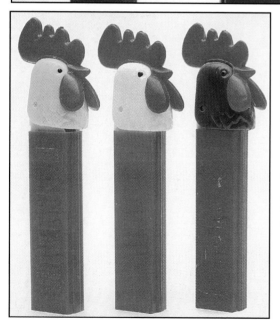

Rooster

Mid-1970s, No Feet
There are several different color variations with white being the most common followed by yellow and green.

White:	**$40-$50**
Yellow or Green:	**$65-$85**

Several color variations can be found of the Rooster—white is the most common. (Green-head rooster from the Maryann Kennedy collection)

Yappy Dog

Mid-1970s, No Feet and With Feet
This head was also used to make Cow B.

Orange head:	**$60-$75**
Green head:	**$70-$85**
With Feet:	**$50-$65**

CHAPTER 4
Disney

BAMBI

Bambi

Late 1970s, No Feet and With Feet
The same mold was used for the Rudolf dispenser but with a red nose (see **HOLIDAY**). A rare version of this dispenser, although subtle, carries the copyright symbol along with the letters "WDP" on the head which can at least double the value.

No Copyright, No Feet:	**$45-$60**
No Copyright, With Feet:	**$35-$45**
With Copyright, No Feet:	**$125-$150**

Bambi, from the late 1970s. The same mold was used to make the Rudolph dispenser.

Bambi's companion Thumper, also from the late 1970s.

Thumper

Late 1970s, No Feet and With Feet
A very subtle yet pricey variation of this dispenser has the copyright symbol along with the letters "WDP" on the head.

No Feet, No Copyright:	**$85-$100**
With Feet:	**$60-$80**
With Copyright:	**$200+**

Chip, from the late 1970s.

Chip

Late 1970s, No Feet and With Feet
PEZ® only produced one half of the famous Disney chipmunk duo of Chip and Dale.

No Feet:	$75-$100
With Feet:	$50-$75

Daisy Duck, from the late 1990s.

Daisy Duck

Late 1990s, With Feet
Daisy is a relatively recent addition to the PEZ® Disney line-up.

Value: $1-$2

Dalmatian Pup

Late 1970s, No Feet and With Feet

No Feet:	$75-$95
With Feet:	$60-$75

Dalmatian pup, from the late 1970s.

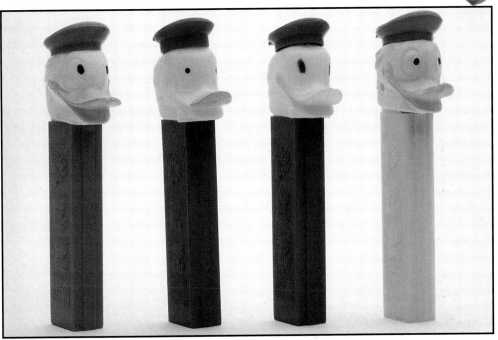

Donald Duck. (L to R) Original Version, Version B, (notice the hole in the beak, also used as Scrooge McDuck head), Version C, and remake Version A.

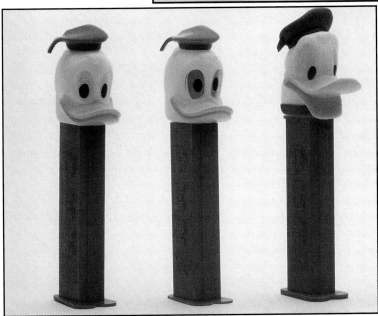

More versions of Donald Duck. (L to R) Version E, with light blue eyes, Version E with dark blue eyes, Version F (current).

Donald Duck

Early 1960s-Current, No Feet and With Feet

Many versions of Donald have been made over the years. Version D, which has holes in the beak, was also used as the head of the Uncle Scrooge McDuck dispenser. An extemely rare "soft-head" version also exists, but these never made it to general production.

Version A, (original-early 1960s) sharp, defined feathers, No Feet:	**$20-$30**
Version B, a remake of A with the feathers less defined on top of head, No Feet:	**$15-$25**
Version C, 2 hinge-holes on the side of the head, milky white plastic head, early-mid-1970s, No Feet and With Feet:	**$15-$25**
Version D, 2 hinge-hole on the side of the head, hole in beak, No Feet and With Feet:	**$10-$20**
Version E, produced in the 1980s, came with both light and dark blue eyes:	**$2-$4**
Version F, late 1990s version, the beak is open:	**$1-$2**
Softhead version:	**$3000+**

Duck Nephews

Originals are from the late 1970s, footed versions are from the late 1980s to 1990s. Variations can be found of this dispenser with large and small pupils. The early version is also known as "Duck Child" and was only produced with blue or green hats; the later versions were produced with red hats, in addition to blue and green.

Originals: **$30-$40**
With Feet: **$5-$10**

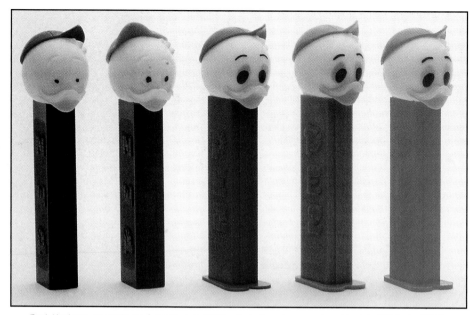

Duck Nephews, originals are from the late 1970s, footed versions are from the late 1980s to 1990s.

Ducktails

Early 1990s, With Feet
Gyro Gearloose: **$5-$8**
Bouncer Beagle: **$5-$8**
Webagail or Webby: **$5-$8**

Ducktails, from the early 1990s. (L to R) Gyro Gearloose, Bouncer Beagle, and Webagail or Webby.

Dumbo, from the late 1970s.

Dumbo

Late 1970s, No Feet and With Feet
No Feet: **$50-$60**
With Feet: **$30-$50**
A very rare softhead
   version also exists: **$3000+**

Goofy, Version B with several face color variations.

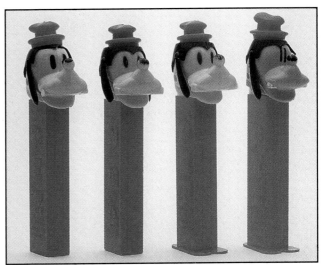

Goofy, Version C with several face color variations.

Goofy

1970s to current, No Feet and With Feet
Several Goofy dispensers have been produced over the years. Versions A, B, and C can be found with several face color variations.

**Goofy A, removable ears, teeth
  and nose, No Feet:** $30-$45
**Goofy B, removable ears and
  teeth, No Feet:** $25-$35
Goofy C, removable ears, No Feet: $25-$35
Goofy C, With Feet: $15-$25
**Goofy D, late 1980s, green hat,
  With Feet:** $2-$5
Goofy E, Current: $1-$2

*Goofy
Version D
(left) and
Version E.*

Unusual variations of Goofy. (From the Johann Patek collection)

25

JUNGLE BOOK

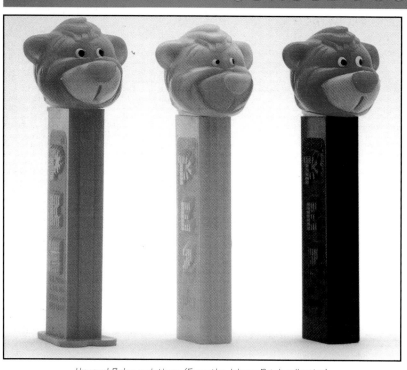

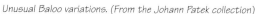

Baloo from the Jungle Book series, released late 1960s.

Unusual Baloo variations. (From the Johann Patek collection)

Baloo

Late 1960s, No Feet and With Feet

Although difficult to find, Baloo was also produced with a yellow or red head.

Blue-gray head, No Feet:	**$30-$40**
Blue-gray head, With Feet:	**$20-$30**
Red or Yellow head, No Feet:	**$300+**

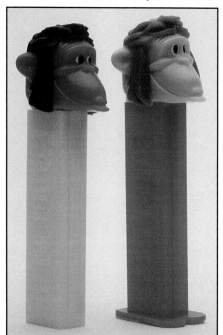

Rare and unusual color variations of King Louie. (From the Maryann Kennedy collection)

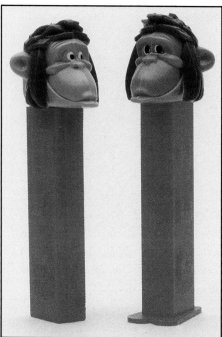

King Louie, from the late 1960s.

More unusual variations of King Louie. (From the Johann Patek collection)

King Louie

Late 1960s, No Feet and With Feet

No Feet:	**$30-$45**
With Feet:	**$25-$35**
Rare and unusual color variations:	**$300+**

Mowgli

Late 1960s, No Feet and With Feet
No Feet: $30-$40
With Feet: $25-$35

Mowgli, from the late 1960s.

Lil Bad Wolf

Mid-1960s, No Feet and With Feet
No Feet: $30-$50
With Feet: $20-$35

Lil Bad Wolf, from the mid-1960s.

Mary Poppins, from the early 1970s. This painted cheek version is extremely rare. (From the Maryann Kennedy collection)

Mary Poppins

Early 1970s, No Feet
This dispenser is very difficult to find. As pictured, an even harder to find "painted cheek" variation. One rumor has it this dispenser was in early production when Disney didn't approve the likeness causing PEZ® to halt further distribution, making this a true rarity!
Value: $850-$1000
Painted cheeks: $950-$1100

Mickey Mouse with "removable nose" or version A, from the early 1970s. The nose piece was also used as Popeye's pipe!

Mickey Mouse B from the early 1980s, and Mickey Mouse C (far right) from the 1990s.

Mickey and Minnie Mouse, late 1990s edition.

Mickey Mouse

Early 1960s-Present, No Feet and With Feet
Mickey Mouse has been one of the most popular PEZ® dispensers over the years and has gone through many variations.

Die-cut stem with painted face, early 1960s:	$300-$400
Die-cut face, early 1960s, No Feet:	$100-$140
Version A, removable nose, early 1970s, No Feet:	$20-$30
Version B, molded nose, early 1980s, No Feet:	$15-$25
Version B, With Feet:	$10-$15
Version C, stencil eyes, 1990s:	$2-$3
Mickey and Minnie Mouse, 1990s edition:	$1-$2
Softhead version (rare):	$3000+

Rare variations of the painted face Mickey Mouse. It is argued that the painted face Mickey Mouse (pictured far left) is the first character head to appear on a dispenser base. This version does not have an applied copyright, and only two are known to exist like this. (From the Johann Patek collection)

Rare test mold of Mickey Mouse. (From the Johann Patek collection)

Mickey Mouse with die-cut face, also from the early 1960s.

Mickey Mouse die-cut with painted face, from the early 1960s. This is the rarest of all Mickey Mouse dispensers. (From the Maryann Kennedy collection)

PETER PAN

Captain Hook

Late 1960s, No Feet
A very rare softhead version of this dispenser was produced in the late 1970s, but never went into general production.

Value: $100-$140
Softhead: $3000+

Captain Hook, from the late 1960s.

Peter Pan, from the late 1960s.

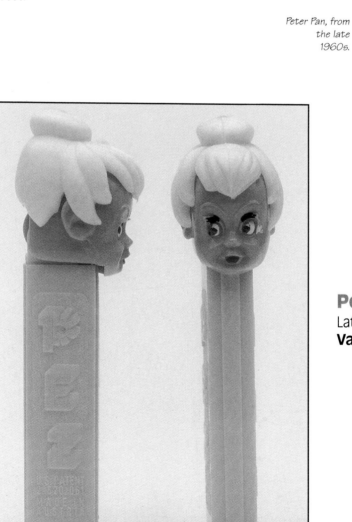

Peter Pan

Late 1960s, No Feet
Value: $175-$225

Tinkerbell

Late 1960s, No Feet
Value: $200-$250

Tinkerbell, from the late 1960s.

PINOCCHIO

Jiminy Cricket, from the early 1970s. He is commonly found to be missing pieces, making this dispenser tough to find complete.

Jiminy Cricket

Early 1970s, No Feet

With many small pieces making up his costume, Jiminy Cricket is a tough dispenser to find complete.

Value: $200-$250

Pinocchio B, from the early 1970s.

Pinocchio

Early 1960s, No Feet

Two versions of Pinocchio were made—one in the early 1960s and the other in the early 1970s. The earlier version (A) can be found with either a red or yellow hat.

Value Version A: $175-$225
Version B: $140-$165

Pinocchio A, from the early 1960s. Can be found with either a red or yellow hat.

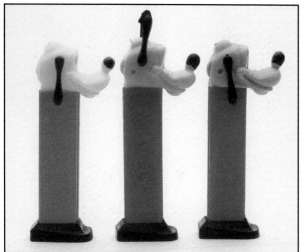

Pluto, first appeared in the early 1960s. (L to R) Original "Hong Kong" Version, Original Version, and caramel color variation of the original.

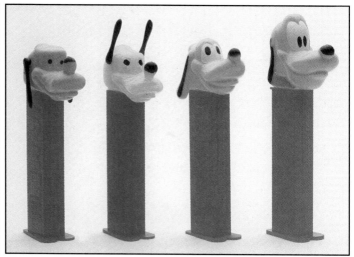

Pluto, the two on the left are Version B and are sometimes called the "flat-head version," Version C is second from right, and on the far right Version D (Current).

Pluto

Early 1960s-Current, No Feet and With Feet

Several versions of Pluto, Mickey Mouse's faithful dog, have been produced through the years.

**Version A, round head
  and movable ears, No Feet:**
                                      $25-$30
Version A, "Hong Kong": $20-$25
**Version B, flat head
  and movable ears:** $10-$15
Version C, molded ears: $2-$5
Version D, (Current): $1-$2

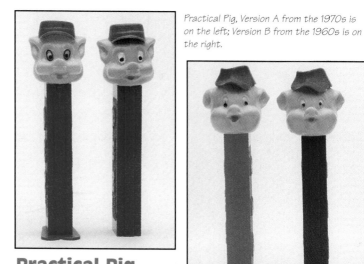

Practical Pig, Version A from the 1970s is on the left; Version B from the 1960s is on the right.

Practical Pig

1960s, No feet and With Feet

Two versions were produced—the earlier version (version A) has a flat hat and the later version (B) produced in the 1970s, has a wavy hat.

Version A, No Feet: $35-$50
Version A, With Feet: $25-$35
Version B, No Feet: $40-$60
Version B, With Feet: $30-$40

Scrooge McDuck

Late 1970s, No Feet and With Feet

The original version used the same mold that was used for Donald Duck Version B, with the glasses, sideburns and hat as separately molded pieces (and easily lost). The remake version has molded sideburns.

Original, No Feet: $30-$40
Original, With Feet: $25-$35
Remake version: $5-$8

Scrooge McDuck, Original version on the left is from the late 1970s; Remake version is on the right.

Disney softheads. Ultra rare and never sold to the public. The few that are known to exist have come from former PEZ® employees. Shown here are Goofy, Donald, and Pluto. (From the Maryann Kennedy collection)

Disney Softheads were never produced for the general public and the heads were never put on stems. The stems here are for display purposes. (From the Dora Dwyer collection)

Disney Softheads

Late 1970s

These dispensers are ultra rare and were never sold to the public. The few that are known to exist have come from former employees of PEZ®. There are six dispensers in this group: Mickey Mouse, Pluto, Goofy(s), Donald Duck, Captain Hook, and Dumbo.

Value:
$3000+ each

SNOW WHITE

Dopey
Late 1960s, No Feet
Value: $200-$225

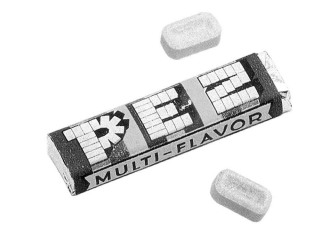

Dopey from the late 1960s.

Snow White
Late 1960s, No Feet
Collar color variations include white, yellow, turquoise, and green. Turquoise is worth slightly more.
Value: $200-$225

Several color variations of the Snow White dispenser. (Dispenser on far left from the Maryann Kennedy collection)

Winnie the Pooh remakes. Came out in 2001 and can be found in several minor variations such as the line/no line version of Eeyore (pictured) and gray/no gray paint on the back of the necks of Tigger and Piglet.

Winnie the Pooh

Late 1970s, No Feet and With Feet
This dispenser was initially released only in Europe. Winnie the Pooh has been quite popular among collectors in general, causing his price to more than double the last few years. Remade and re-released in the summer of 2001, Winnie the Pooh and friends can now be found in the U.S.

No Feet:	$75-$100
With Feet:	$65-$85
Remakes:	$1-$3

Winnie the Pooh, released in the late 1970s but not in the U.S.

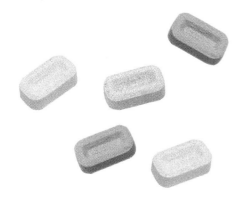

Zorro

1960s, No Feet
This dispenser can be found in several different versions: small and large logo and variations of the hat and mask. Some versions have a curved mask and others have a straight mask.

Versions with logo: $100-$125
Non-logo: $75-$100

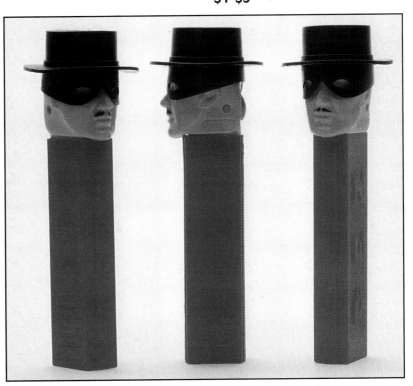

Zorro, from the 1960s. The dispenser in the center has the "Zorro" logo stem.

CHAPTER 5

Guns

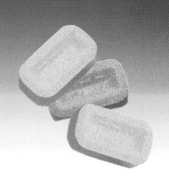

The half acrylic version on the top was used to test the internal workings during production. The acrylic portion would be fitted to a randomly selected gun by a factory worker and checked to make sure the mechanisms worked properly. (From the Johann Patek collection)

Front and back of candy shooter mint on card. (From the Johann Patek collection)

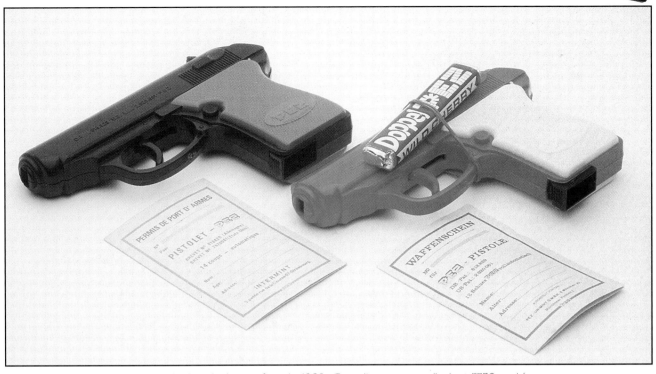

Black and red candy shooters from the 1960s. These dispensers actually shoot PEZ® candy!

Candy Shooters

Mid-1960s

These dispensers actually shoot PEZ® candy! Candy shooters can be found in black and red as well as blue, green, and orange. The blue and green guns are very difficult to find and command much higher prices.

Brown: $100-$140   **Red or Orange:** $65-$85   **Blue or Green:** $300-$350

A Candy Shooter on its original card—very difficult to find. (From the Maryann Kennedy collection)

An earlier version of the Candy Shooter card that never had a gun mounted on it. (From the Maryann Kennedy collection)

Backside of the Candy Shooter card with a target for kids to cut out and take aim.

WOW! European PEZ factory early 1950s.

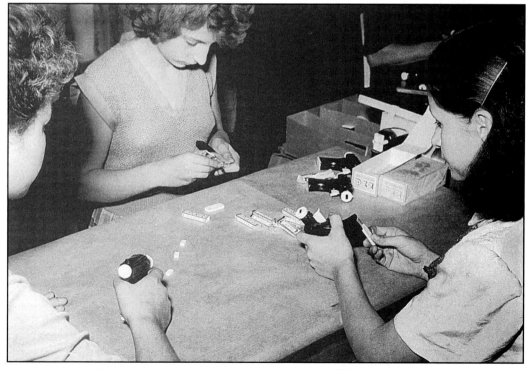

Test firing the space gun. Notice the old candy packs have the 'PEZ box' regular on the back.

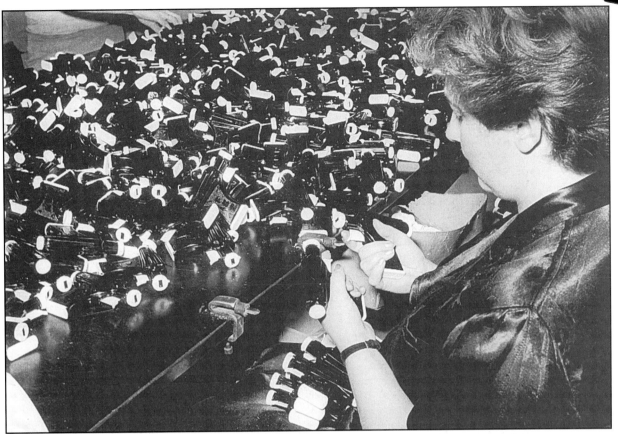

Space Guns

1950s

Space guns also shoot PEZ® candy and are very desirable among collectors. They were offered as a mail-in premium as well as sold in stores until the mid-1960s. They can be found in 11 different colors: red, yellow, green, black, blue, maroon, light blue, lavender, silver, gold, and transparent.

Red, Yellow, or Green:	**$500-$600**
Black or Blue:	**$550-$650**
Maroon:	**$850-$950**
Light Blue, Lavender, Gold, or Silver:	**$2000+**
Transparent (few known to exist):	**$3000+**

Space guns from the 1950s on the original counter display card. Each card originally held six guns. A very rare item, especially in this condition. (From the Maryann Kennedy collection)

An assortment of 1950s space guns.

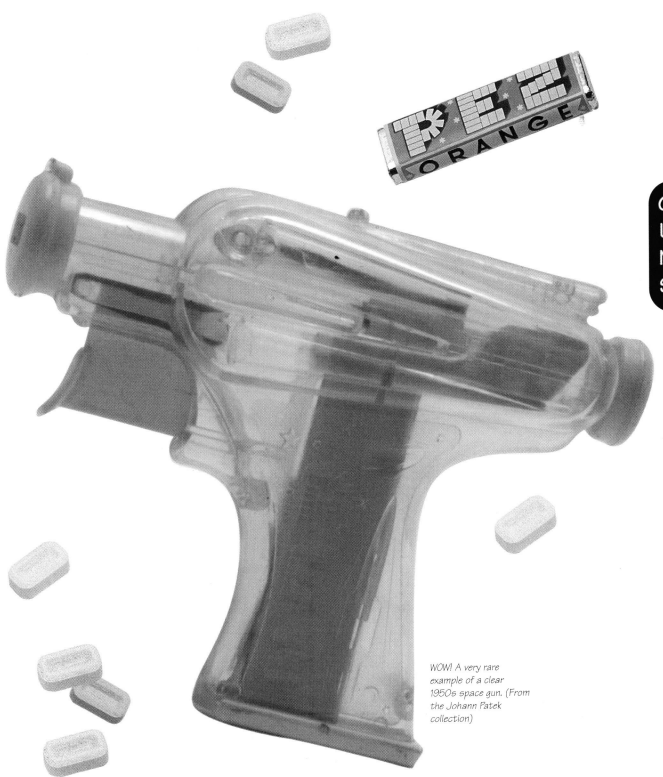

WOW! A very rare
example of a clear
1950s space gun. (From
the Johann Patek
collection)

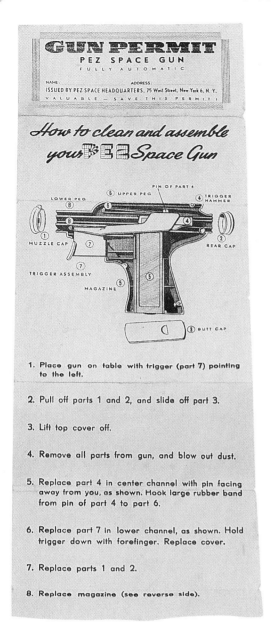

This 1950s space gun permit is valued at $30 to $40.

A very difficult to find premium offer featuring the 1950s space gun. This 3 panel sheet has the following inscription inside; "A PEZ GUN FREE OF CHARGE- Collect 136 Pez wrappers and stick them onto the squares designed for this purpose. When the folder is filled hand it in to your dealer or send it directly to the address cited on the last side. Your effort will pay. In turn, you will obtain a span-new Pez gun free of charge which to possess you will be envied by all your friends." ("Span-new" is an actual typo) $200+.

1980s Space Gun

PEZ® produced another space gun in the 1980s to capitalize on the space craze caused by the *Star Wars* movies. Two versions exist, a Hong Kong version and an Austrian version.

Silver Space Gun:	**$100-$150**
Red Space Gun:	**$85-$125**

1980s silver space gun.

1980s red space gun.

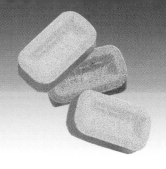
CHRISTMAS

Unusual Angel variations, the one on the left is the "loop" version and the one on the right has removable eyes, yellow hair, and a larger than normal halo. (From the Johann Patek collection)

Angel

Early 1970s, No Feet and With Feet
Several versions of the angel have been produced, including one with a small plastic loop on the back of her hair that allows it to be used as an ornament.

No Feet:	**$85-$100**
With Feet:	**$50-$65**
Unusual blond hair	
version:	**$90-$125**
Ornament:	**$100-$125**

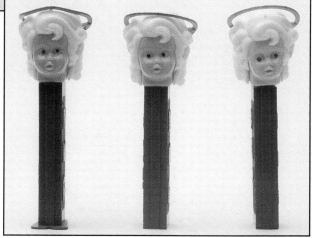

Three versions of the Angel dispenser. (L to R) Yellow hair with feet, yellow hair without feet, and a rare blond version.

Icee Bear

1990s, With Feet
The earlier version of Icee Bear was not issued in the U.S. The version on the far right made its debut in the 1999 Christmas assortment. It was revised in 2002.

Early Version,
  left and center: **$5-$10 each**
Far right: **$1-$3**
(Current version is pictured on page 48)

Icee Bear. The one on the left and in the middle was not issued in the U.S. The version on the right debuted in the 1999 Christmas assortment.

Rudolph

Late 1970s, No Feet and With Feet
The mold used to produce Bambi was also used for Rudolph—but the nose on Rudolph was painted red.
No Feet: **$50-$75**
With Feet: **$35-$50**

Rudolph was made from the same mold as the Bambi dispenser—but Rudolph's nose was painted red.

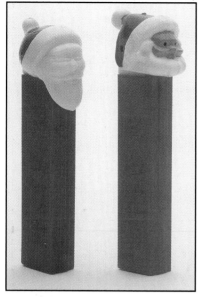

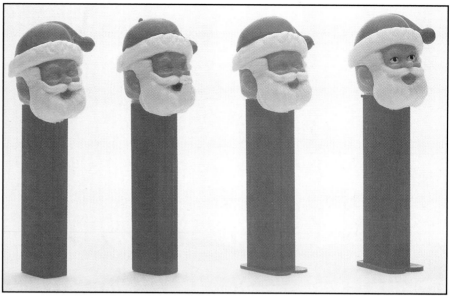

Santa A (on the left), from the late 1950s;
Santa B (right), from the 1960s.

Santa C. This is a VERY common dispenser. From left to right, Version C no feet; Version C with loop on the back of his hat to be used as an ornament; Version C with feet; and Version D.

Full Body Santa, from the 1950s. This version of St. Nick measures approximately 3 1/2" from boots to hat and is very popular with collectors.

Full Body Santas in the original counter box! This box is very difficult to find and few are known to exist. Also pictured is an original insert that came rubber-banded around each Santa. The insert had instructions for loading the dispenser and an offer for a Golden Glow. Box: $200-$250; Insert: $20-$30.

Santa

1950s-Present, No Feet and With Feet
Santa is one of the most popular PEZ® dispensers ever produced. Most commonly found is Santa C, which has been produced since the 1970s.

Santa A, No Feet, face and beard are the same color:	**$120-$150**
Santa B, No Feet, flesh-colored face with white beard:	**$125-$160**
Santa C, No Feet:	**$5-$10**
Santa C, With loop for ornament:	**$35-$50**
Santa C, With Feet:	**$2-$3**
Santa D, With Feet:	**$1-$2**
Santa E, (Current):	**$1-$2**
Full Body Santa (1950s):	**$150-$200**

A jolly assortment of Santa dispensers.

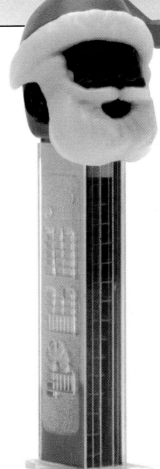

*Rare variations
of 'ole St. Nick.
(From the
Johann Patek
collection)*

New Christmas holiday dispensers released Fall of 2002: Santa, Snowman, Winter Bear, Elf, and Reindeer.

Holiday 2002
With Feet:
$1-$2 each

Snowman
1970s, No Feet and With Feet
No Feet: $15-$25
With Feet: $1-$5
"Misfit" versions (mail-in offer, late 1990s): $5-$8

The Snowman first appeared in the 1970s. The two dispensers on the far right are "Misfit" versions from the late 1990s.

EASTER

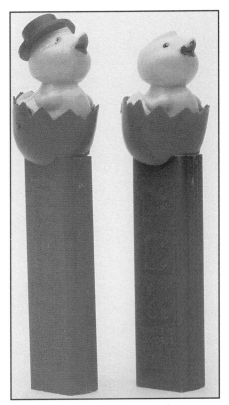

On the left is the Chick in Egg A with hat old version with thin, brittle shell. Notice the steel pin. On the right is the Chick in Egg, no hat, this is the oldest version.

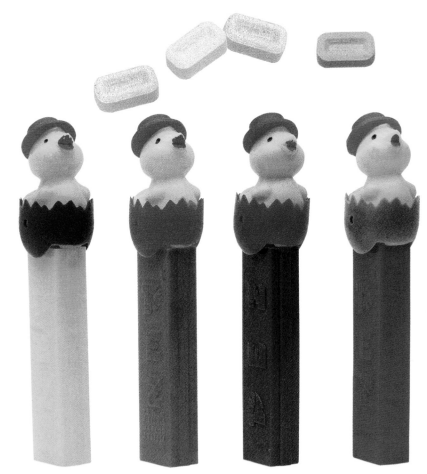

Chick in Egg B with hat, from the 1970s. This second version has a thin flexible plastic shell with more uniform points that resemble a saw blade.

Chick in Egg

Early 1970s-Current, No Feet and With Feet
The earliest versions of this popular dispenser have a brittle plastic eggshell with jagged points. The second version has a thin flexible plastic shell with more uniform points that resemble a saw blade. The third version, from the 1980s, has a much thicker shell but with the same type of points as on the second version. The current version is also a thicker plastic but there are fewer points on the shell and edges are more rounded.

Chick in Egg, No Hat, No Feet: $85-$120
Chick in Egg A, With Hat, No Feet: $75-$100
Chick in Egg B, With Hat, No Feet: $15-$25
Chick in Egg C, With Hat, No Feet: $10-$15
Chick in Egg C, With Hat, With Feet: $5-$10
Chick in Egg D, With Hat, With Feet: $2-$3
Chick in Egg E, With Hat, With Feet (Current): $1-$2

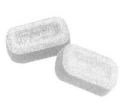

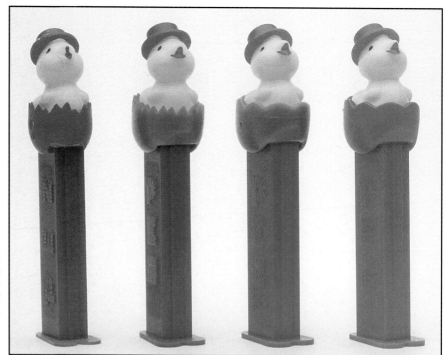

More recent versions of the Chick in Egg with hat from the 1980s to current. The dispenser on the far left is Version B with feet, Version C is next to that, and the two on the right are Version D.

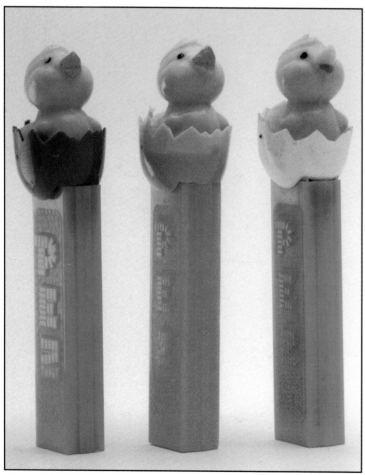

Three variations of the Chick in Egg without hat. (From the Johann Patek collection)

Chick on Easter card. The graphics make this piece very desirable: $150-$200. (From the Maryann Kennedy collection)

Easter Bunny

1950s-Current, No Feet and With Feet

Bunny A, No Feet, 1950s:	**$200-$250**
Bunny B, No Feet, 1950s:	**$250-$300**
Fat Ear Bunny, No Feet,	
1960s-1970s:	**$25-$40**
Fat Ear Bunny, With Feet:	**$10-$20**
Bunny D, 1990s:	**$2-$4**
Bunny E, (Current):	**$1-$2**

Easter Bunny. (L to R) Bunny A from the 1950s; Fat ear bunny from the 1960s and 1970s; Bunny D from the 1990s; and Bunny E Current.

Bunny B from the 1950s. This is a tough one to find. (From the Maryann Kennedy collection)

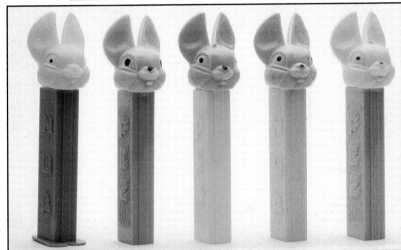

Various fat ear bunnies. These can be found in many different shades.

New crystal holiday dispensers - lamb, chick, rabbit, and panda. Only available through mail order. $3-$5 each

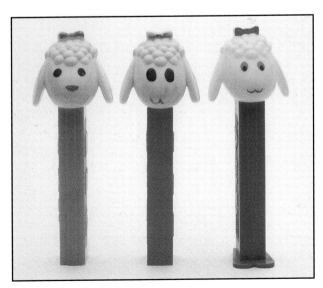

Lamb

1970s, No Feet and With Feet

No Feet:	**$20-$30**
With Feet:	**$1-$3**

Three versions of the lamb dispenser.

HALLOWEEN

The Halloween crystal series was released in 1999 through a PEZ® mail- in offer.

Halloween ghosts, the U.S. version from 1999-2001. These do not glow in the dark.

Halloween Crystal Series

1999, With Feet
This series was only available through a PEZ® mail-in offer. The series includes a Jack-o-Lantern and three different ghosts.
Value: **$3-$5 each**

Halloween Ghosts

Late 1990s, With Feet
This non-glowing series was available in the U.S. for only a couple of years. Characters include: Naughty Neil, Slimy Sid, and Polly Pumpkin. These do not glow in the dark.
Value: **$1-$2 each**

Halloween glowing ghosts. From left to right: Happy Henry, Naughty Neil, Slimy Sid, and Polly Pumpkin.

They actually glow in the dark!

Halloween Glowing Ghosts

Late 1990s, With Feet
This glowing version first sold only in Europe, not released in the U.S. assortment until 2002. Characters include: Happy Henry, Naughty Neil, Slimy Sid, and Polly Pumpkin.
Value: **$1-$2 each**

They glow!

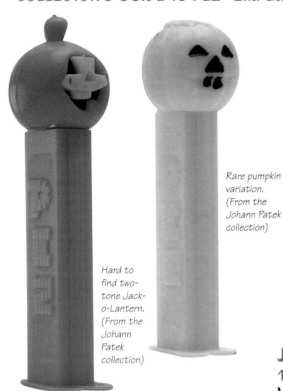

Rare pumpkin variation. (From the Johann Patek collection)

Hard to find two-tone Jack-o-Lantern. (From the Johann Patek collection)

Jack-o-Lantern. From left to right, Version A; Version A with feet; Version B; and Version C.

Jack-o-Lantern
1980s, No Feet and With Feet

Version A, die-cut face, No Feet:	**$20-$25**
Version A, With Feet:	**$10-$15**
Version B:	**$2-$3**
Version C:	**$1-$2**
Version D glows in the dark (current):	**$1-$2**

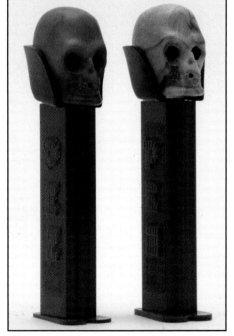

Rare marbelized Skull variations. (From the Johann Patek collection)

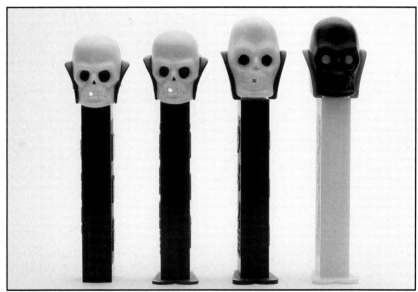

Skull. From left to right, Version A; Version A with feet; Version B with larger head; and "Misfit" Version.

Skull
Early 1970s-Current, No Feet and With Feet

A "misfit" version of the skull with a black head was available in 1998 through a mail-in offer. A very hard to find variation of version B is known as the "Colgate" skull because he has a full set of teeth!

Version A, No Feet:	**$15-$20**	**Version B, glows in the dark:**	**$1-$3**
Version A, With Feet:	**$10-$15**	**"Misfit" version:**	**$5-$8**
Version B, larger head:	**$1-$3**	**Full set of teeth:**	**$50-$60**

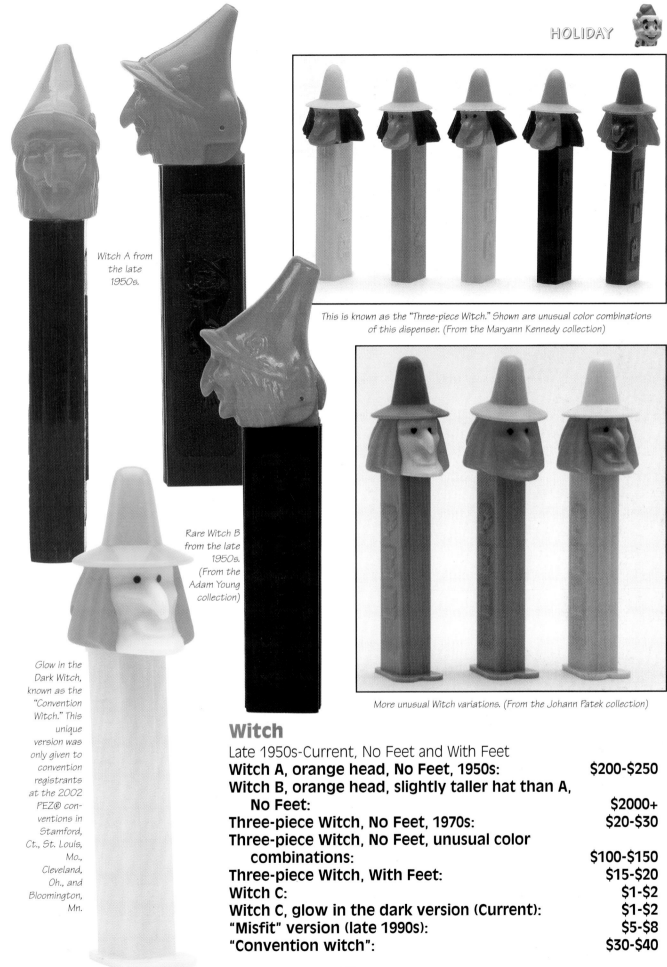

Witch A from the late 1950s.

This is known as the "Three-piece Witch." Shown are unusual color combinations of this dispenser. (From the Maryann Kennedy collection)

Rare Witch B from the late 1950s. (From the Adam Young collection)

Glow in the Dark Witch, known as the "Convention Witch." This unique version was only given to convention registrants at the 2002 PEZ® conventions in Stamford, Ct., St. Louis, Mo., Cleveland, Oh., and Bloomington, Mn.

More unusual Witch variations. (From the Johann Patek collection)

Witch

Late 1950s-Current, No Feet and With Feet

Witch A, orange head, No Feet, 1950s:	**$200-$250**
Witch B, orange head, slightly taller hat than A, No Feet:	**$2000+**
Three-piece Witch, No Feet, 1970s:	**$20-$30**
Three-piece Witch, No Feet, unusual color combinations:	**$100-$150**
Three-piece Witch, With Feet:	**$15-$20**
Witch C:	**$1-$2**
Witch C, glow in the dark version (Current):	**$1-$2**
"Misfit" version (late 1990s):	**$5-$8**
"Convention witch":	**$30-$40**

More common versions
of the Three-piece
Witch from the 1970s.

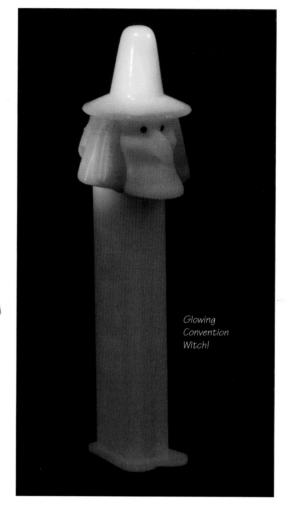

Glowing
Convention
Witch!

More Witches. (L to R) Three-piece Witch with
feet; Witch C, with unusual patent marking on
side of stem; two "Misfit" versions.

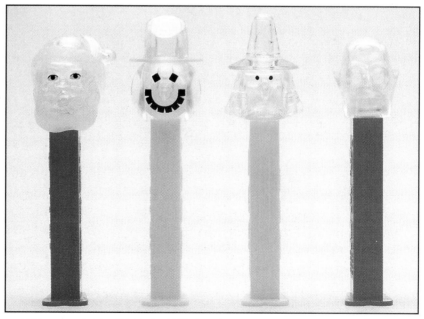

Holiday Crystal Series

1999, With Feet

This series was only available
through a PEZ® mail-in offer. The
series includes Santa, Snowman,
Witch, and Skull.

Value: $3-$5 each

Holiday crystal series. Released in 1999 through a PEZ® mail-in offer, and featured Santa,
Snowman, Witch, and Skull dispensers.

VALENTINE'S DAY

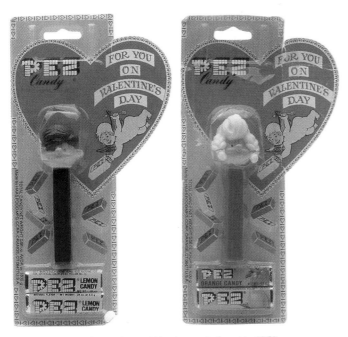

Boy and Girl on die-cut Valentine cards from the 1970s.

Boy and Girl on Valentine cards from the late 1980s/early 1990s.

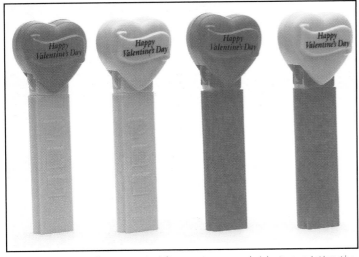

Valentines hearts. The two on the left are a very unusual pink stem variation; the other two are common.

Current Valentine hearts on cards.

Valentine

1970s-current, No Feet and With Feet

Boy and Girl PEZ® Pals on die-cut Valentine cards, No Feet, 1970s: $150-$200 each

Boy and Girl PEZ® Pals on Valentine cards, With Feet, late 1980s/early 1990s: $15-$20 each

Valentine hearts, red stem, No Feet: $1-$3

Valentines hearts, unusual pink stem, No Feet: $125-$150

CHAPTER 7

Humans

Rare variation of Astronaut 2. (From the Johann Patek collection)

Rare Astronaut 1 variation. Notice the smooth helmet. (From the Johann Patek collection)

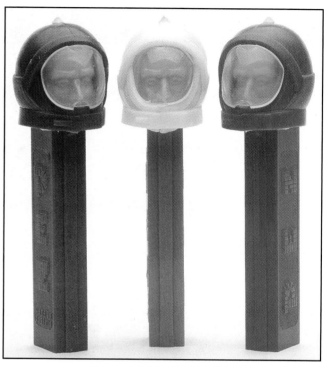

Astronaut 2, from the late 1970s.

The stem inscription from the rare "World's Fair Astronaut." (From the Dora Dwyer collection)

Astronaut 1, from the early 1960s. This dispenser was not released in the U.S, and can also be found with a white or light blue helmet. (From the Maryann Kennedy collection)

Astronaut

Early 1960s, No Feet

The Astronaut 1 was not released in the U.S., but the second Astronaut, released in the 1970s was distributed in the U.S. A very rare version of this dispenser exists and is known as the "World's Fair Astronaut" because of the inscription on the left side of the stem. Only two of these dispensers are known to exist—one with a green stem and white helmet and the other with a blue-green stem and matching helmet.

Astronaut 1:	**$600-$700**
Astronaut 2 white helmet/green stem:	**$125-$150**
Astronaut 2 blue helmet/blue stem:	**$140-$160**
World's Fair Astronaut:	**$3000+**

★★★★★ BICENTENNIAL ★★★★★

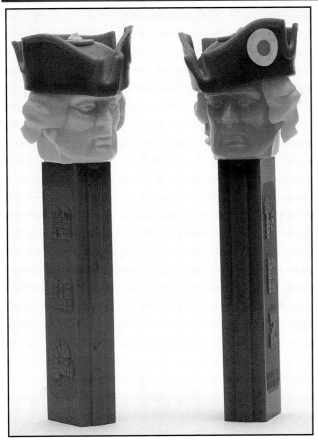

Captain, also known as Paul Revere. He should have the sticker on the left side of his hat as shown to be considered complete.

Betsy Ross
Mid-1970s, No Feet
Value: $125-$150

Captain
(Also known as Paul Revere)
Mid-1970s, No Feet
This dispenser should have a sticker on the left side of his hat to be considered complete.
Value: $150-$175

Daniel Boone
Mid-1970s, No Feet
Value: $175-$200

Betsy Ross (above) and Daniel Boone (left) from the Bicentennial series released in 1975.

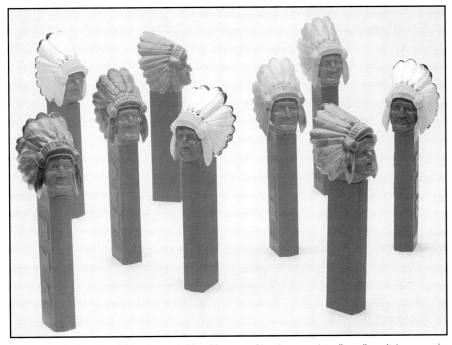

Indian Chiefs, from the 1970s. The swirled headdress combinations are virtually endless. It is rumored the plastic used to make the headdress was molded from the ground up, re-melted remains of unsold Make-a-Face dispensers.

Indian Chief
Early-1970s, No Feet
The swirled headdress combinations are virtually endless. It is rumored the plastic used to make the headdress was molded from the ground up and re-melted remains of unsold Make-a-Face dispensers.
Value: $125-$150
White headdress: $100-$125

H
U
M
A
N
S

The Indian Brave (L) was released in the early 1970s. The Indian Maiden (R) was part of the Bicentennial series released in 1975.

Indian Brave
Early-1970s, No Feet
Value: **$150-$175**

Indian Maiden
Mid-1970s, No Feet
Value: **$125-$150**

Pilgrim from the Bicentennial series released in 1975.

Pilgrim
Mid-1970s, No Feet
The Pilgrim can be found with either a white or yellow hatband.
Value: **$125-$150**

Wounded Soldier from the Bicentennial series released in 1975.

Uncle Sam
Mid-1970s, No Feet
Value: **$175-$200**

Wounded Soldier
Mid-1970s, No Feet
Value: **$125-$150**

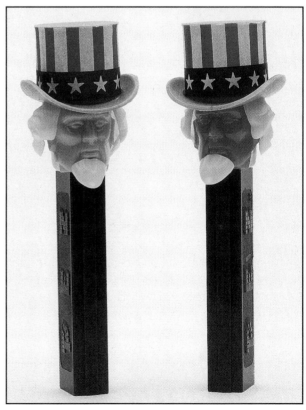

Uncle Sam, part of the Bicentennial series released in 1975.

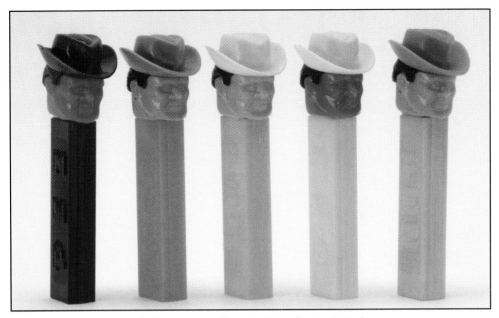

Cowboy variations. (From the Johann Patek collection)

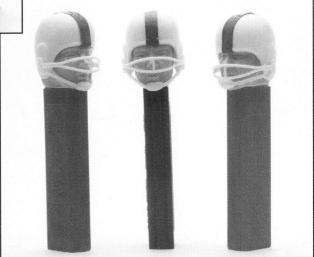

Cowboy, from the early 1970s.

Cowboy
Early 1970s, No Feet
Value: **$200-$250**

Football Player with original vending box.

Football Player
Mid-1960s, No Feet
This dispenser can be found in either red or blue and will either have a tape strip on the helmet (as shown) or a plastic strip that snaps on the front and back of the helmet. This version is very tough to find. The blank side of the stem with the triangle allowed kids to customize the dispenser with a pennant-shaped sticker of their favorite team.
Tape-strip Helmet: **$150-$175**
Snap-on Stripe: **$250+**

Football Player, from the mid-1960s. Notice the unique stem—the blank side with the triangle allowed kids to customize the dispenser with a pennant-shaped sticker of their favorite team.

Pilot and Stewardess
Mid-1970s, No Feet

Pilot: $175-$200
Stewardess: $175-$200

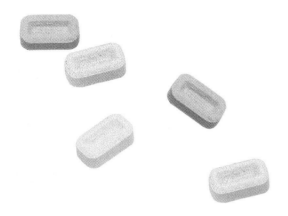

Pilot and Stewardess, from the mid-1970s.

Spaceman
Late 1950s, No Feet

A premium version of the Spaceman was offered by Cocoa Marsh in the late 1950s. The premium version had "Cocoa Marsh" on the stem. Several stem variations include light blue, dark blue, and metallic blue, as well as clear or transparent blue helmet.

Value: $150-$175
Cocoa Marsh Spaceman: $175-$225

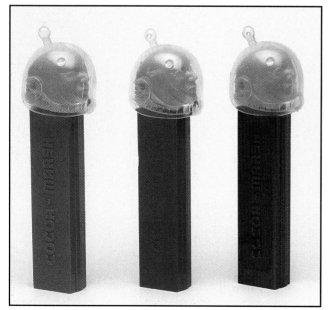

Cocoa Marsh spaceman dispenser offered as mail-in premium in the 1950s. Cocoa Marsh was chocolate flavored syrup "milk booster."

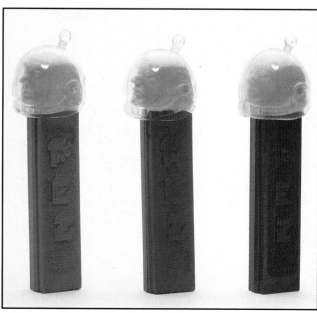

Spaceman dispenser, from the late 1950s. Same as the Cocoa Marsh spaceman except this one has the PEZ® logo on both sides.

CHAPTER 8

Licensed Characters

Annie
Early 1980s, No Feet
Released to coincide with the release of the movie *Annie*. The movie wasn't a hit and neither was the dispenser, making this one a little tough to find.
Value: **$150-$175**

ASTERIX

Asterix is a popular European comic. These dispensers have not been released in the U.S. The series was first produced by PEZ® in the mid-1970s and a remake of the original series was released in the late 1990s. The remakes have feet and painted on eyes. The Roman Soldier was not included in the original series.

Annie, released early 1980s around the movie Annie.

Asterix
Mid-1970s, No Feet and With Feet
Original: **$1500-$2000**
Remake: **$3-$5**

Muselix
Mid-1970s, No Feet and With Feet
Original: **$2500-$3000**
Remake, called "Getafix"
by PEZ: **$3-$5**

Obelix
Mid-1970s,
No Feet and With Feet
Original: **$1500-$2000**
Remake: **$3-$5**

Roman Soldier
Late 1990s, With Feet
Value: **$3-$5**

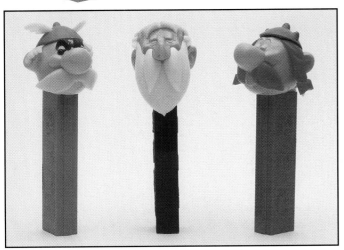

Asterix series, originally released in the mid-1970s. (L to R) Asterix, Muselix, Obelix. (Asterix and Obelix from the Maryann Kennedy collection)

Remake of the Asterix series. (L to R) Obelix, Muselix (sometimes called "Getafix"), Asterix, and Roman Soldier.

Bob the Builder series released in 2002: Bob, Wendy, Pilchard the Cat, and Spud the Scarecrow.

Bob the Builder

2002, With Feet
Value: $2-$4

Bozo the Clown, from the early 1960s.

Bozo the Clown

Early 1960s, No Feet
This dispenser is usually die-cut on the side of the stem with a picture of Bozo and Butch. The non-die-cut stem is actually more difficult to find.
Die-cut Stem: $175-$200
Plain Stem: $185-$225

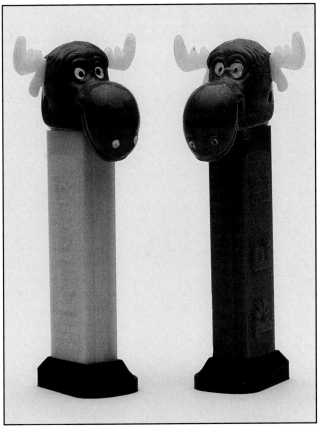
Bullwinkle, from the early 1960s. The brown stem version on the right is much harder to find than the yellow stem version.

Bullwinkle
Early 1960s, No Feet
Bullwinkle can be found with either a yellow or a brown stem—the brown is much harder to find.
Yellow Stem: $250-$275
Brown Stem: $275-$325

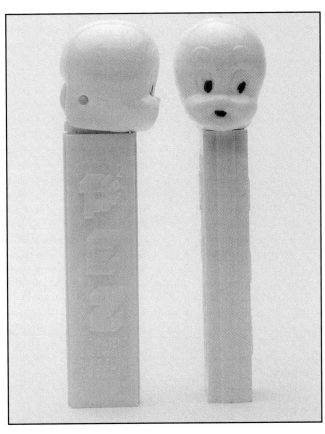

Harvey Cartoon character Casper the Friendly Ghost, from the late 1950s.

Casper
Late 1950s, No Feet
No one is sure which licensed character first graced the top of a PEZ® dispenser. Some say it was Mickey Mouse, some say Popeye, and others say Casper. One story has it that Curt Allina, executive vice-president of PEZ® from 1953 to 1979, and Mr. Harvey, creator of Casper, had apartments in the same New York building in the 1950s. While living there the two developed a friendship and an agreement to use Harvey's character on the candy dispenser. The rest, as they say, is history.
Casper can be found with white, light blue, and light yellow stems as well as a die-cut version with a red or black sleeve.
Value: $150-$175
Die-cut Stem: $200-$250

Phone home, it's E.T.! Came out with the summer 2002 movie re-release.

E.T.
2002, With Feet
Value: $1-$3

That modern stone-age family – The Flintstones. (L to R) Fred, Barney, Pebbles, and Dino.

Flintstones

Mid-1990s, With Feet
Series includes Barney Rubble, Dino, Fred Flintstone, and Pebbles Flintstone.
Value: **$1-$2**

A rare test mold version of Garfield. (From the Johann Patek collection)

Garfield 1st Series. (L to R) Garfield, Garfield with teeth, Garfield with visor, Arlene, and Nermal (two versions).

Garfield 2nd Series. (L to R) Garfield, Chef Garfield, Sleepy Garfield, Aviator Garfield, and Odie.

Garfield

1990s, With Feet
Two series featuring the comic strip character Garfield have been produced—the first in the early 1990s, the second in the late 1990s. The first series includes Garfield, Garfield with teeth, Garfield with visor, Arlene, and Nermal. The second series includes Garfield, Chef Garfield, Sleepy Garfield, Aviator Garfield, and Odie.
First Series: **$2-$3 each**
Second Series: **$1-$2 each**

MGM CHARACTERS

Barney Bear, an MGM character released in the early 1980s.

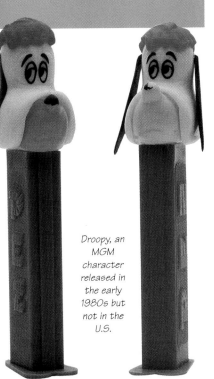

Droopy, an MGM character released in the early 1980s but not in the U.S.

Barney Bear
Early 1980s, No Feet and With Feet

No Feet:	**$35-$45**
With Feet:	**$20-$30**

Droopy
Early 1980s, No Feet and With Feet
This dispenser was not released in the U.S. Two versions were made—one with painted ears and one with movable ears.

Painted ears:	**$3-$8**
Moveable ears:	**$20-$25**

Jerry, from the early 1980s to current. (L to R) No Feet, Thin Feet, Multi-Piece Face, With Feet, and the Current release.

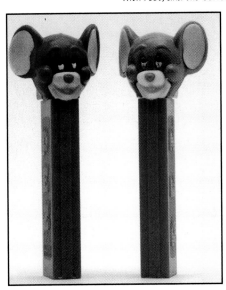

Rare ear insert versions of Jerry and Tuffy. (From the Johann Patek collection)

Variations of the multi-piece face Jerry.

Jerry
Early 1980s to current, No Feet and With Feet
One half of MGM's famous cat and mouse duo. Not released in the U.S. There are MANY variations to this dispenser.

No Feet:	**$30-$40**
Thin Feet:	**$5-$10**
Multi-piece face:	**$10-$15**
With Feet:	**$4-$8**
Current:	**$2-$3**

67

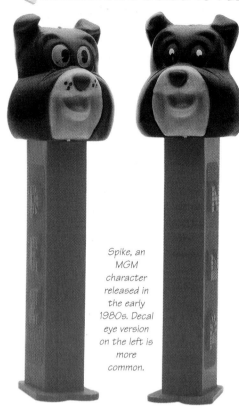

Spike, an MGM character released in the early 1980s. Decal eye version on the left is more common.

Spike

Early 1980s, No Feet and With Feet
Spike was not released in the U.S. Several versions exist including small painted eyes, decal eyes, and an unusual variation with a green head.

Decal eyes:	**$5-$10**
Small painted eyes:	**$15-$20**
Green head:	**$100-$125**

Tom, an MGM character first released in the early 1980s.

Tom

Early 1980s, No feet and With Feet
The feline portion of MGM's famous cat and mouse pair. Not released in the U.S. Several versions have been produced.

No Feet:	**$25-$35**
With Feet:	**$3-$8**
Multi-piece Face:	**$5-$10**

Tuffy, an MGM character first released in the early 1990s.

Tuffy

Early 1990s, With Feet
A non-U.S. release, Tuffy looks very similar to Jerry but has gray face instead of brown.

Painted Face:	**$3-$5**
Multi-piece Face:	**$10-$15**
Current:	**$2-$4**

Tyke, an MGM character first released in the early 1980s.

Tyke

Early 1980s, No Feet and With Feet
Non-U.S. release.

Small Painted Eyes:	**$25-$35**
Decal Eyes:	**$15-$20**

THE MUPPETS

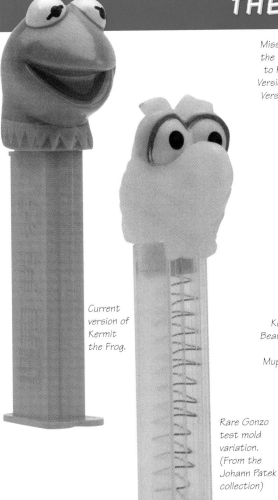

Current version of Kermit the Frog.

Miss Piggy from the Muppets. (L to R) "Eyelash" Version, Common Version, Current Release.

Kermit, Fozzie Bear, and Gonzo from the Muppets series.

Rare Gonzo test mold variation. (From the Johann Patek collection)

Muppets

Early 1990s, With Feet
Included in the series are Fozzie Bear, Gonzo, Kermit the Frog, and Miss Piggy. A harder to find version with eyelashes exists of Miss Piggy.

Miss Piggy With Eyelashes:	**$10-$15**
Miss Piggy (common and current versions):	**$1-$3**
Fozzie, Gonzo, and Kermit:	**$1-$2**

Nintendo series. (L to R) Diddy Kong, Yoshi, Koopa Trooper, and Mario.

Nintendo

Late 1990s, With Feet
A series not available in the U.S. featuring characters from Nintendo's video games. Dispensers include Diddy Kong, Yoshi, Koopa Trooper, and Mario.

Value: $2-$3 each

LICENSED CHARACTERS

PEANUTS CHARACTERS

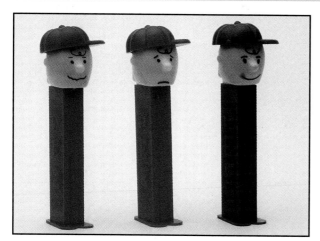

Charlie Brown from the Peanuts series. (L to R) Smiling, Frowning, With Tongue Showing.

Lucy from the Peanuts series. (L to R) Common Version, White around Eyes, White Face (Psycho Lucy).

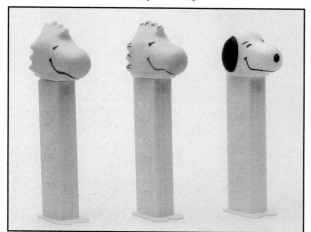

Woodstock and Snoopy from the Peanuts series. The Woodstock with Feathers is in the center.

Peanuts 2000. (L to R) Charlie Brown, Lucy, Snoopy, and Woodstock.

Peanuts

Early 1990s to current, With Feet

Characters include Charlie Brown, Lucy, Snoopy, Woodstock, and Peppermint Patty. Several variations exist for each.

Charlie Brown, smiling:	**$1-$2**
Charlie Brown, frowning (non-U.S.):	**$5-$10**
Charlie Brown, tongue showing (non-U.S.):	**$5-$10**
Charlie Brown, eyes closed (non-U.S.):	**$50-$60**
Lucy, common version:	**$1-$2**
Lucy, white around eyes:	**$50-$75**
Lucy, white face (known as "psycho Lucy"):	**$75-$90**
Peppermint Patty:	**$1-$2**
Snoopy:	**$1-$3**
Snoopy as "Joe Cool":	**$1-$3**
Woodstock, common version:	**$1-$2**
Woodstock with feathers (black markings on the top and back of his head):	**$3-$5**

Peppermint Patty and Joe Cool released fall of 2000.

Peter PEZ®

Late 1970s, No Feet and With Feet
A dispenser featuring the clown mascot of the PEZ® Candy company. The original was produced in the late 1970s and a remake came out in the early 1990s.

Original version, No Feet:	**$75-$85**
Remake (1993 to 2001):	**$2-$4**
Current:	**$1-$2**
"Rico" variation:	**$20-$30**

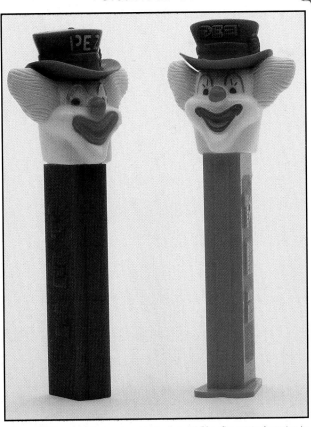

Peter PEZ®, originally appeared in the late 1970s. The original version is on the left, and the remake from the 1990s is on the right.

Peter PEZ® "Rico" variation. "Rico" means candy.

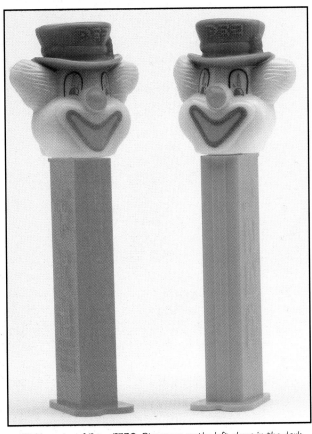

2001 version of Peter PEZ®. Dispenser on the left glows in the dark (mail order only).

LICENSED CHARACTERS

Pink Panther

Late 1990s, With Feet
Not available in the U.S., this series featured the Pink Panther, Inspector Clouseau, Ant, and Aardvark.

Value: **$2-$3 each**
2002 remake: **$2-$5**

Pink Panther series, released in the late 1990s. (L to R) Pink Panther, Inspector Clouseau, Ant, and Aardvark.

2002 version of Pink Panther.

Pokémon

2001, With Feet
Value: **$1-$4**

Pokémon dispensers released in 2001. (L to R) Pikachu, Meowth, Mew, Psyduck, and Koffing.

Popeye

Late 1950s to late 1970s, No Feet

Some believe Popeye was the first licensed character PEZ® ever used on a dispenser. Brutus and Olive Oyl were produced in the mid-1960s and usually are found with missing or chipped paint on their faces.

Popeye, original version, hat is molded to the head:	**$150-$175**
Popeye B, plain face:	**$125-$150**
Popeye C, with pipe (note the pipe is the same piece used on Mickey Mouse's nose):	**$100-$125**
Brutus:	**$250-$275**
Olive Oyl:	**$275-$325**

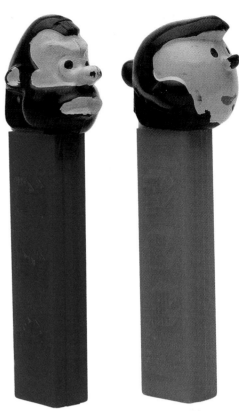

Brutus and Olive Oyl, from the mid-1960s.

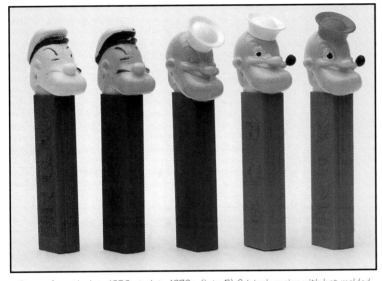

Popeye, from the late 1950s to late 1970s. (L to R) Original version with hat molded to head (2 examples), Version B, Version C with removable pipe (2 examples).

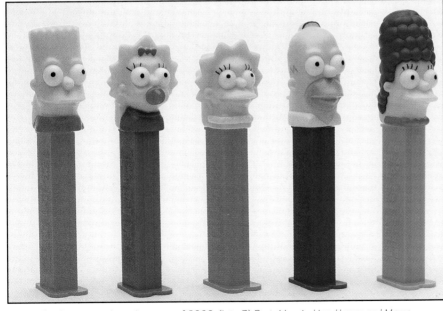

The Simpsons, released summer of 2000. (L to R) Bart, Maggie, Lisa, Homer, and Marge.

Simpsons

Spring 2000, With Feet

Doh! It's the whole Simpson family! Bart, Maggie, Lisa, Homer, and Marge.

Value: $1-$2 each

LICENSED CHARACTERS

Smurfs, original series from the late 1980s including Smurf, Papa Smurf, and Smurfette.

Jango Fett, R2-D2 and Clone Trooper. R2-D2 is only the second dispenser to have the entire body on top of the dispenser!

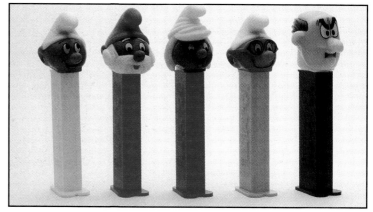

Smurfs, current series, released late 1990s. (L to R) Smurf, Papa Smurf, Smurfette, Brainy Smurf, and Gargamel.

Smurfs

Late 1980s, No Feet and With Feet

Two Smurf series were produced—one in the late 1980s and the second in the late 1990s. Series one included Smurf, Smurfette, and Papa Smurf. The second series includes Smurf, Papa Smurf, Smurfette, Brainy Smurf, and Gargamel.

Smurf (1st series), No Feet:	**$10-$15**
(1st series), With Feet:	**$5-$10**
Smurfette (1st series), No Feet:	**$10-$15**
(1st series), With Feet:	**$5-$10**
Papa Smurf (1st series), No Feet:	**$10-$15**
(1st series), With Feet:	**$5-$10**
Second Series:	**$3-$5 each**

Star Wars

Late 1990s, With Feet

PEZ® released three series of dispensers featuring characters from the *Star Wars* universe. The first series included five dispensers: Darth Vader, Stormtrooper, C3-PO, Yoda, and Chewbacca. The second series, released summer of 1999 included: Ewok, Princess Leia, Boba Fett, and Luke Skywalker. The third series released summer 2002 in conjunction with the movie *Attack of the Clones* featured Jango Fett, R2-D2, and Clone Trooper.

Value (all series):	**$1-$3 each**

Star Wars. Top Row: Stormtrooper, Darth Vader, Stormtrooper. Center Row: Ewok, Princess Leia, Boba Fett, Yoda. Bottom Row: Luke Skywalker, Chewbacca, C-3PO.

Teenage Mutant Ninja Turtles—Smiling Version. (L to R) Leonardo, Michelangelo, Donatello, and Raphael.

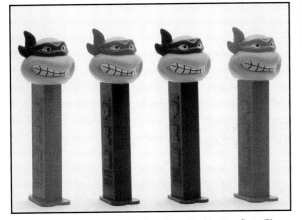

Teenage Mutant Ninja Turtles—Frowning Version. (L to R) Leonardo, Michelangelo, Donatello, and Raphael.

Teenage Mutant Ninja Turtles

Mid-1990s, With Feet

Two series were produced—a smiling version and an angry version of Leonardo, Michelangelo, Donatello, and Raphael. With 8 different turtle heads and 8 stem colors, collecting all variations presents a bit of a challenge.

Smiling version: **$2-$3 each**
Angry version: **$2-$3 each**

Tweenies released summer 2002. (L to R) Jake, Fizz, Milo, Bella, and Doodles. These are the first actual dispensers to have painted stems!

Tweenies

2002, With Feet
Released in Europe summer of 2002.
Value: **$2-$4**

WARNER BROTHERS CHARACTERS

Bugs Bunny, from the late 1970s to current. (L to R) No feet, With Feet and older style head (2 examples), Painted ears, and Current style.

Bugs Bunny

Late 1970s to current, No Feet and With Feet

No Feet:	**$15-$20**
With Feet, older style head:	**$5-$10**
Painted Ears:	**$1-$2**
Current:	**$1-$2**

L
I
C
E
N
S
E
D

C
H
A
R
A
C
T
E
R
S

Daffy Duck, from the late 1970s to current. The version on the far left is toughest to find with the separate eye pieces.

Cool Cat, a Warner Brothers character, released in the early 1980s.

Daffy Duck

Late 1970s to current, No Feet and With Feet
Many versions of Daffy have been produced. The first version with separate eye pieces is the toughest to find.

Daffy Duck A (separate eye pieces):	**$25-$30**
Daffy Duck B (painted eyes and tongue):	**$15-$20**
Daffy Duck C (with feet, older style head):	**$5-$8**
Daffy Duck D (current style):	**$1-$2**

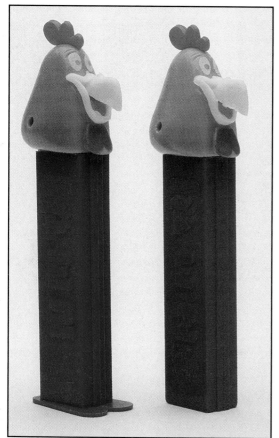

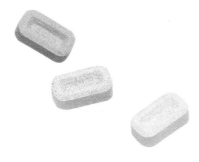

Cool Cat

Early 1980s, No Feet and With Feet
A rare "slim face" version also exists.

No Feet:	**$65-$85**
With Feet:	**$45-$65**
Slim Face:	**$100+**

Foghorn Leghorn

Early 1980s, No Feet and With Feet
Foghorn Leghorn can be found with either a yellow or an orange beak. A rare "slim head" version also exists.

No Feet:	**$85-$100**
With Feet:	**$65-$85**
Slim Head:	**$100+**

Foghorn Leghorn, a Warner Brothers character, from the early 1980s.

Merlin Mouse, a Warner Brothers character, from the early 1980s.

Henry Hawk, a Warner Brothers character, released in the early 1980s.

Henry Hawk

Early 1980s, No Feet and With Feet

No Feet: $80-$100
With Feet: $60-$75

Merlin Mouse

Early 1980s, No Feet and With Feet

No Feet: $20-$30
With Feet: $12-$15

Petunia Pig

Early 1980s, No Feet and With Feet

No Feet: $40-$50
With Feet: $30-$40

Petunia Pig, a Warner Brothers character, dispenser first appeared in the early 1980s.

L
I
C
E
N
S
E
D

C
H
A
R
A
C
T
E
R
S

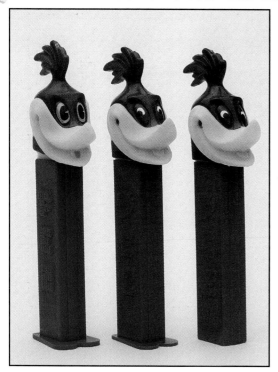

Roadrunner, Warner Brothers character, from the early 1980s.

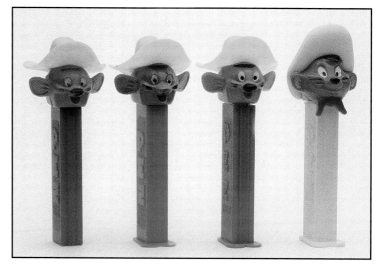

Speedy Gonzales, a Warner Brothers character, from the late 1970s to current.

Roadrunner

Early 1980s, No Feet and With Feet

Painted eyes, No Feet:	**$30-$40**
Painted eyes, With Feet:	**$25-$30**
Stencil eyes, With Feet (this is the most common version):	**$20-$25**

Speedy Gonzales

Late 1970s to current, No Feet and With Feet

No Feet:	**$30-$40**
With Feet, older head:	**$15-$25**
Current:	**$1-$2**

Sylvester, a Warner Brothers character, first released in the late 1970s. (L to R) No Feet, With Feet and older style head, With feet and whiskers (black lines under nose), Current (2 variations).

Sylvester

Late 1970s, No Feet and With Feet
Several versions of Tweety Bird's nemesis exist.

No Feet:	**$15-$20**
With Feet, older style head:	**$5-$8**
With Feet, with whiskers (black lines under nose), non-U.S. version:	**$4-$8**
Current:	**$1-$2**

Tazmanian Devil

Late 1990s, With Feet

Value:	**$1-$2**
Cycling Taz (with hat):	**$1-$2**

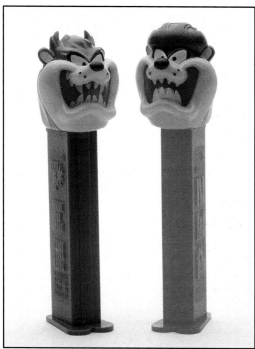

Tazmanian Devil and Cycling Taz, released late 1990s.

Tweety

Late 1970s to Current, No Feet and With Feet
The oldest version is hardest to find; it has separate pieces for the eyes (known as removable eyes).

Removable eyes, No Feet:
$20-$25
Painted eyes, No Feet: $15-$20
Painted eyes, With Feet: $3-$5
Current: $1-$2

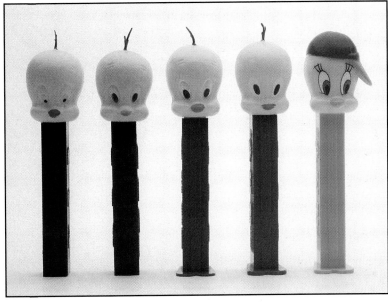

Tweety, a Warner Brothers character, first appeared in the late 1970s to current. The version on the far left is hardest to find. It has separate pieces for the eyes (known as removable eyes).

Wile E. Coyote, a Warner Brothers character, first appeared in the early 1980s.

Wile E. Coyote

Early 1980s, No Feet and With Feet
A rare "slim head" version can also be found.

No Feet: $45-$65
With Feet: $35-$45
Slim Head: $100+

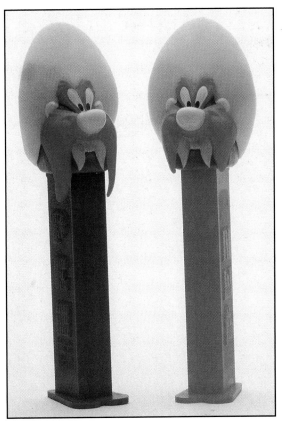

Yosemite Sam, a Warner Brothers character, released in the mid-1990s. The U.S. version is on the left.

Yosemite Sam

Mid 1990s, With Feet
The shorter mustache on the non-U.S. version allows body parts to put on the dispenser.
U.S. Version: $1-$2
Non-U.S. Version: $2-$4

Eerie Specters, also known as "soft-head" monsters. These are from the late 1970s and very popular among collectors. There are two variations: "Made in Hong Kong" and "Hong Kong." The later of the two is a bit harder to find. There is also a very distinct difference in face color between the two. The back row is the "Hong Kong" version. The stems of these dispensers are always marked, "Made in the USA."

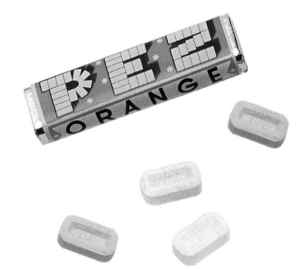

Air Spirit (made in Hong Kong version is on the left).

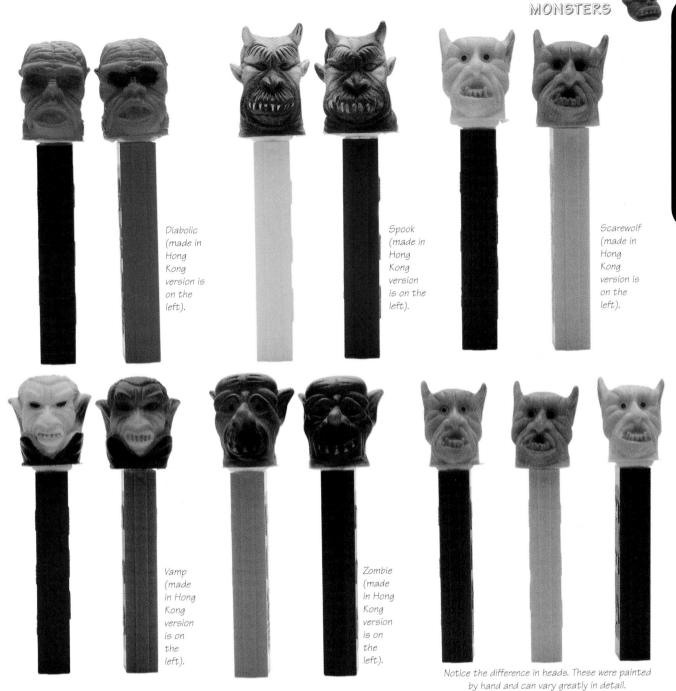

Diabolic (made in Hong Kong version is on the left).

Spook (made in Hong Kong version is on the left).

Scarewolf (made in Hong Kong version is on the left).

Vamp (made in Hong Kong version is on the left).

Zombie (made in Hong Kong version is on the left).

Notice the difference in heads. These were painted by hand and can vary greatly in detail.

Eerie Specters
(Also known as Softhead Monsters)

Late 1970s, No Feet

This group is very popular among collectors. There are two variations for each character—"Made in Hong Kong" and "Hong Kong." These are the two different markings used on the back of the head with the "Hong Kong" mark being a bit harder to find. There is also a very distinct difference in face color between the two. The stems of these dispensers are always marked "Made in the USA." The six characters in the series are Air Spirit, Diabolic, Scarewolf, Spook, Vamp, and Zombie.

"Made in Hong Kong":	**$200-$250**
"Hong Kong":	**$225-$275**

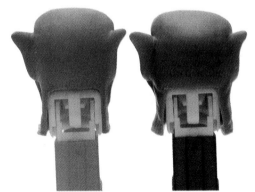

Identifying marks on the back of the head.

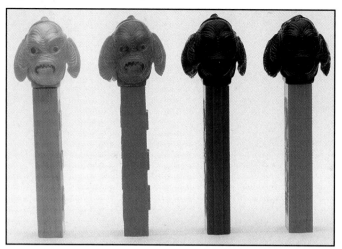

The all green version on the far left is known as the Creature from the Black Lagoon, or just the Creature. The others are referred to as the "Fishman." The Creature, from the mid-1960s, has a very unique "pearl-essant" stem that matches the head.

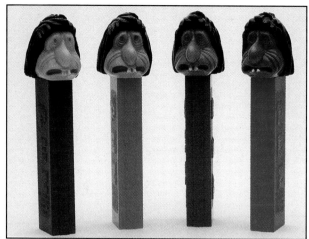

Mr. Ugly, from the early 1970s, with several head-color variations. (L to R): chartreuse green, aqua-green, and olive green.

Fishman

Mid-1970s, No Feet

The Fishman used the same mold as the Creature from the Black Lagoon, which was done as part of a Universal Studios Monsters series. The Creature was all green whereas the Fishman came with either a green or a black head and various colored stems.

Value: $175-$200

Mr. Ugly

Early 1970s, No Feet and With Feet

This really is a homely guy! Several variations to the face coloring exist and differ in value.

Chartreuse green face:	**$75-$95**
Aqua green face:	**$80-$90**
Olive green face:	**$60-$75**
With Feet:	**$45-$65**

One-Eyed Monster

Early 1970s, No Feet and With Feet

This dispenser was available with either an orange, brown, black, gray, pink, or yellow head.

No Feet:	**$80-$100**
With Feet:	**$65-$80**

Universal Studios Monsters

Mid-1960s, No Feet

A highly coveted series among PEZ® collectors and Universal Studio fans. The Creature has a very unique pearlescent stem.

Creature from the Black Lagoon:	**$300-$350**
Wolfman:	**$275-$325**
Frankenstein:	**$275-$325**

One-Eyed Monster, from the early 1970s. Can also be found with brown, gray, pink, or yellow head.

Universal Studios Monsters, from the mid-1960s. (L to R): Wolfman, Creature from the Black Lagoon, and Frankenstein.

CHAPTER 10

PEZ Pals

PEZ® Pals are one of my favorite groups. They are popular among collectors and have a clever concept to boot! Pezi Boy is a detective who dresses up in disguises to solve mysteries. With these various disguises he becomes different characters such as a Policeman, Knight, Sheik, and Doctor. These characters were shown in the Pezi comics—inserts that came packaged with the dispensers in the 1960s.

The characters all used the same head, so the PEZ® Company only needed to produce small, inexpensive accessories to make a whole new dispenser. Kids were encouraged to "collect them all" and interchange the pieces to make their own character. It is easy to understand why many of these dispensers are missing parts.

Admiral

Date Unknown, No Feet
A very rare dispenser, this is the only one currently known to exist. The Admiral character has been shown on various PEZ® advertisements such as comics and candy boxes but none had been found until recently.

Value: $3000+

Alpine Man, from the 1972 Munich Olympics. (From the Maryann Kennedy collection)

Admiral. A very rare dispenser, this is the only one currently known to exist. (From the Silvia Biermayr/Gerhard Trebbin collection)

Alpine Man

Early 1970s, No Feet
Produced for the 1972 Munich Olympics, this is a very rare and difficult dispenser to find.

Value: $1500+

Boy and Boy with Cap

Mid-1960s-current, No Feet and With Feet

Many versions of the PEZ® Pal Boy have been produced through the years. One of the rarest is the brown-hair boy without hat used in a mid-1980s promotion for the movie *Stand By Me*. The dispenser is packaged with one pack of multi-flavor candy and a miniature version of the movie poster announcing the videocassette release and the quote "If I could only have one food to eat for the rest of my life? That's easy, PEZ®. Cherry flavored PEZ®. No question about it." This dispenser must be sealed in original bag to be considered complete.

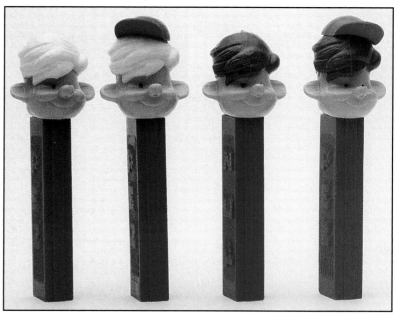

Boy and Boy with cap, from the mid-1960s. Both the blonde and brown-hair versions can also be found with a red hat.

Boy with blue cap, blonde hair:	**$100-$125**
Boy with red cap, blonde hair:	**$250-$300**
Boy with blue cap, brown hair:	**$75-$100**
Blonde Hair:	**$50-$75**
Brown Hair:	**$25-$35**
Stand By Me (sealed in bag with mini-poster):	**$200-$250**

Bride

Late 1970s, No Feet

The Bride is a very rare and much desired piece by collectors. This dispenser, along with the Groom, was created for Robert and Claudia's wedding (relatives of a PEZ® executive) that took place October 6, 1978. They were used as place setting gifts and each guest received a set. The Bride is much harder to find than the Groom. It should be noted that the hair is different than the hair on the nurse.

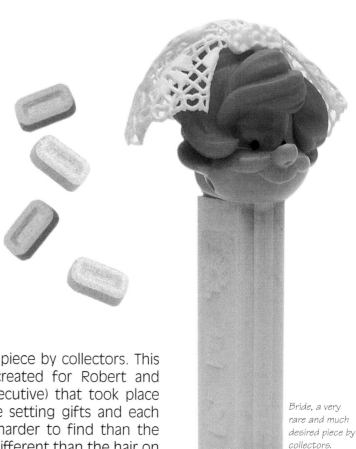

Bride, a very rare and much desired piece by collectors.

Orange Hair:	**$1800-$2000**
Brown Hair:	**$2000-$2200**
Blonde Hair:	**$2100-$2300**

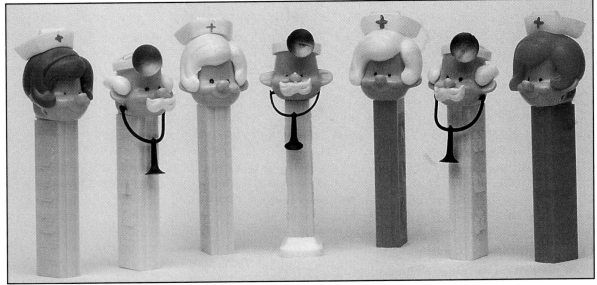

Doctors and Nurses. Both of these dispensers are available in several versions.

Doctor and Nurse

Early 1970s, No Feet

Both of these dispensers are available in several versions. The doctor comes with OR without hair on either a blue, white, or yellow stem. The nurse can be found with brown, reddish orange, yellow, or blonde hair on several different stem colors. There is also a variation in her hat: one is a solid white and the other is an opaque or milky-white, semi- transparent color that is usually only found in dispensers that came from Canada.

Doctor: $150- $250   **Nurse:** $150- $200

Fireman, from the early 1970s. Notice the one on the right has a slightly different color badge.

Engineer

Mid-1970s, No Feet

Value: $175-$200

Fireman

Early 1970s, No Feet

The Fireman was available with a dark moustache. White moustache rarities must be sealed in the package to be considered a variation. Notice the light gray badge variation on the fireman on the far right.

Darker Badge: $75-$90
Lighter Badge: $85-$100

Engineer from the mid-1970s.

Girl

Early 1970s, No Feet and With Feet
The Girl can be found with either blonde or yellow hair.

No Feet: $25-$35
With Feet: $5-$10

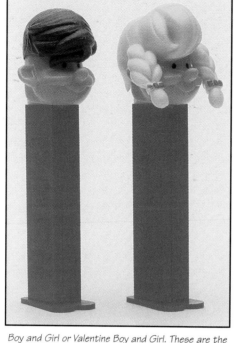

Boy and Girl or Valentine Boy and Girl. These are the most recent version (no hole in nose).

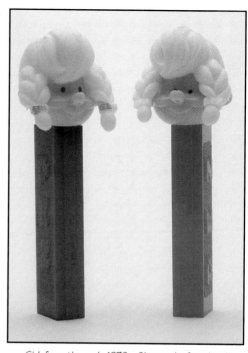

Girl, from the early 1970s. She can be found with blonde or yellow hair.

Groom, a very rare dispenser.

Groom

Late 1970s, No Feet
A rare dispenser from the October 6, 1978 wedding of Robert and Claudia (relatives of a PEZ® executive).

Value: $500-$700

New Limited Edition Bride and Groom (mail order only).

LIMITED EDITION
Bride and Groom

Current, With Feet
New limited edition Bride and Groom dispensers (mail order only).

Value: $30-$45 per set

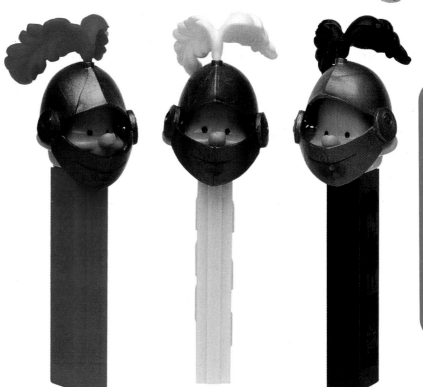

Knight

Early 1970s, No Feet
The Knight was available in three colors—red, black, or white. The white knight is the hardest to find. The plume color on the helmet must always match the stem in order to be correct.

Red: $300-$350
Black: $350-$375
White: $500-$600

Knights—the white knight in the center is the hardest to find.

Maharajah, from the early 1970s. Notice the one on the far left. His turban is shaped slightly different than the other two. This is the "Hong Kong" version; the one in the middle has a darker green turban and the one on the right is the most common of the three.

A rare black variation. (From the Johann Patek collection)

Maharajah

Early 1970s, No Feet
There are several variations to this dispenser. One version, made in Hong Kong, has a slightly different turban than the others.

Hong Kong Version: $75-$85
Darker Green Turban: $80-$100
Lighter Green Turban: $60-$80

87

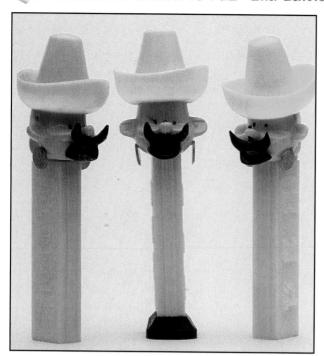

Mexican, from the mid-1960s. This one can be tough to find with all of his pieces.

Mexican

Mid-1960s, No Feet

With removable hat, goatee and earrings, this one can be tough to find with all of his pieces.

Value: $200-$250

1990s PEZ® Pals

Mid-1990s, With Feet

PEZ® introduced a new PEZ® Pals series in the mid-1990s designed specifically to be used with "Body Parts" (see pp. 163-164). Included in the series are a Pilot, Shell Gas Attendant, and Alpine Boy. The series was not sold in the U.S.

Value: $8-$12 each

With matching body parts outfits:
                     $10-$15 each

Glowing Head versions: $5-$10

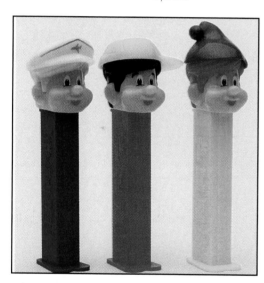

New PEZ® Pal series from the mid-1990s. Left to right: Pilot, Shell Gas attendant, and Alpine boy.

New PEZ® Pals in their matching body parts outfits.

Shell PEZ® Pals with hair color variations. White, Brown, Black, Gray, Silver, and Gold. Black hair is the most common.

They actually glow in the dark!

Mariner and BP PEZ® Pals in matching body parts.

New PEZ® Pals glowing head versions.

Aral PEZ® Pal with hair color variations. (Aral is a gas station in Europe.) Black hair is the most common followed by red and yellow.

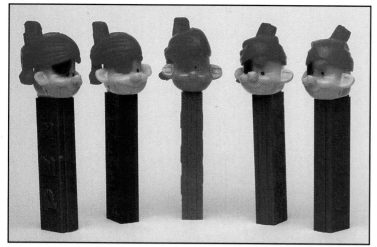

Pirates, from the early 1970s. There are three different variations shown here. The two on the left have a different scarf or bandana than the two on the right. The dispenser in the middle has a flesh tone color variation that is very difficult to find.

Pirate

Early 1970s, No Feet
Variations can be found in the Pirate's bandana and in his skin tone.
Value: **$60-$85**

Policeman, from the early 1970s.

Policeman

Early 1970s, No Feet
Value: **$50-$75**

Ringmaster, from the mid-1970s. It is common to find this dispenser missing his moustache.

Ringmaster

Mid-1970s, No Feet
An uncommon dispenser—and usually found missing his moustache.
Value: **$275-$350**

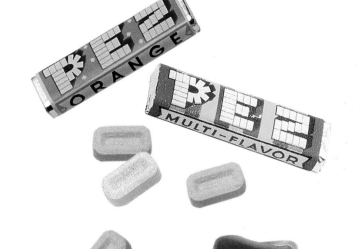

Sailor
Late 1960s, No Feet
Value: **$175-$225**

Sailor, from the late 1960s.

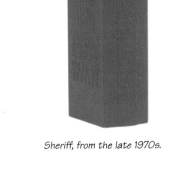

Sheriff, from the late 1970s.

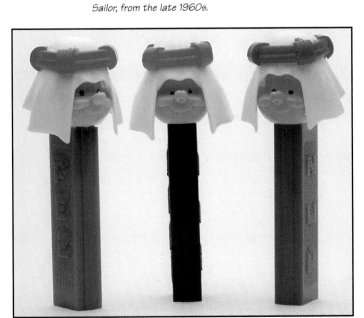

Sheik, from the early 1970s.

Sheik
Early 1970s, No Feet
The Sheik can be found with either a red or black band on top of the burnoose.
Red Band: **$80-$100**
Black Band: **$90-$125**

Sheriff
Late 1970s, No Feet
Value: **$150-$200**

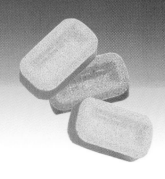

CHAPTER 11

Regulars

The first regular!

Here it is, the ORIGINAL PEZ® regular! This little guy is just over 3/4-inch wide and barely measures 2 1/2-inches tall. It matches the size of the mechanical drawing for patent number 2,620,061 exactly!

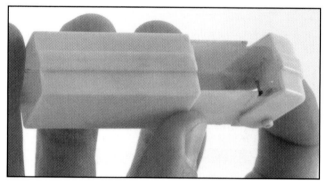

With the sleeve extended.

The opposite side.

The original PEZ® regular. Currently the only one in the world known to exist! It was found in a trash can! (From the Johann Patek collection)

Bosch ad regulars. (From the Johann Patek collection)

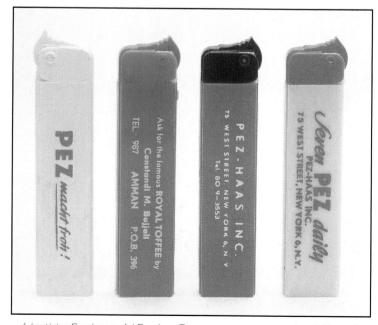

Advertising Regulars or Ad Regulars. These were never mass-produced. (From the Maryann Kennedy collection)

Advertising Regulars or Ad Regulars

These dispensers were never mass-produced. Most were screened one at a time and in very small quantities. They were given to customers and sales reps as "business cards." Ad Regulars are very difficult to find, and from time to time previously unknown ads turn up. The ultra-rare "Lonicot" regular is among the rarest of the Advertising dispensers. Only three are currently known to exist. Lonicot is German for "low nicotine." PEZ® was touted as an alternative to smoking, so for a brief time they experimented with a candy that actually contained nicotine. This is the container that was to dispense that candy. To this date no candy has been found, only the dispenser and a small bit of paper work.

Value: **$1000-$1500 each**
Lonicot Dispenser: **$3000+**

Safeway ad regular. (From the Johann Patek collection)

The ultra-rare "Lonicot" regular. (From the Maryann Kennedy collection)

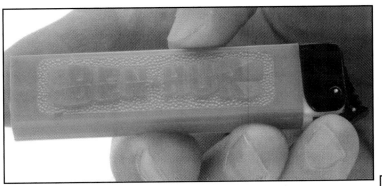

Ben Hur ad regular, currently the only one known. (From the Johann Patek collection)

A variety of Arithmetic dispensers. (From the Johann Patek collection)

Arithmetic Dispensers

Early 1960s
Arithmetic Regulars were available as a mail-in premium as well as sold in stores. They can be found in red, blue, green, tan, and yellow.

Blue:	**$500-$700**
Green:	**$600-$800**
Red:	**$700-$900**
Tan or Yellow:	**$800-$1000**

Arithmetic dispensers were offered as a mail-in premium as well as sold in stores. Shown here with the original insert. (Red dispenser from the Maryann Kennedy collection)

Box Trademark Regular

Late 1940s to early 1950s
Thought to be the first generation of dispenser design.
Value: **$4500+**

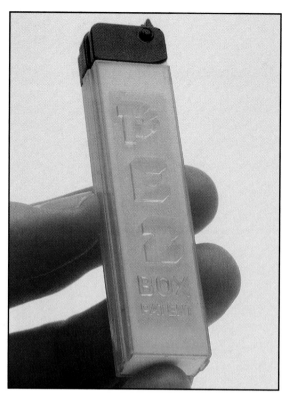

Box trademark regular. (From the Johann Patek collection)

Rare locking cap regular. (From the Johann Patek collection)

Box Patent regular (non-U.S.). A very rare dispenser. (From the Maryann Kennedy collection)

Locking cap regular

Late 1940s
Value: **$4000+**

Box Patent Regular

Early 1950s
This is believed to be the second-generation dispenser design, the Box trademark being the first. It was not sold in the U.S. and is a very rare dispenser.
Value: **$4000+**

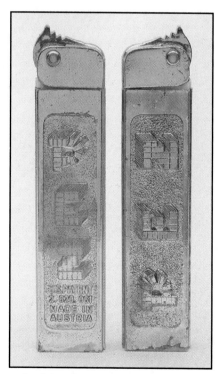

The Golden Glow dispenser was only offered through a mail-in promotion.

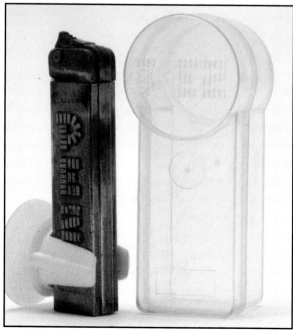

A very rare golden Glow with Lucite case and suction cup holder. (From the Johann Patek collection)

94

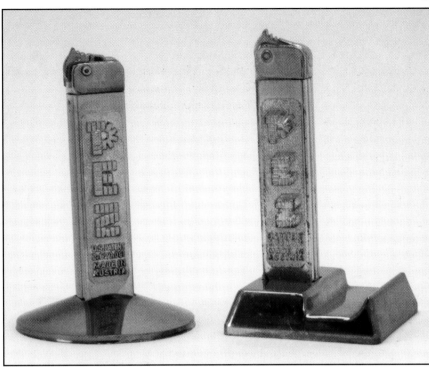

Original Golden Glow still in the package! (From the Johann Patek collection)

Vintage Golden Glows with stands. The round base is the older of the two. (From the Johann Patek collection)

Golden Glow

This dispenser was offered only as a mail-in premium and is tough to find with finish in good condition—tarnish spots are common.

Value: $85-$125

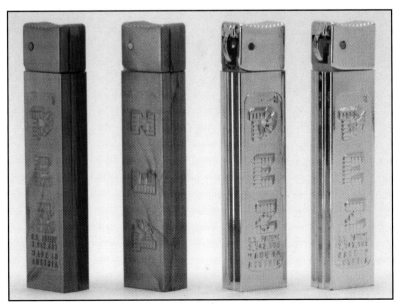

Newer Golden Glow regulars. (From the Johann Patek collection)

New Golden Glow 50th anniversary dispenser! 2002 marks the 50th year of PEZ® in America. To celebrate the milestone, PEZ® re-created this vintage dispenser. One side of the cap is embossed 1952 the other 2002. Sold through a mail order offer for the special price of $19.52!

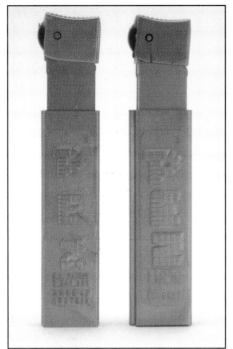

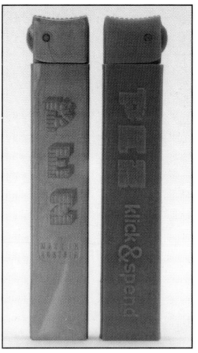

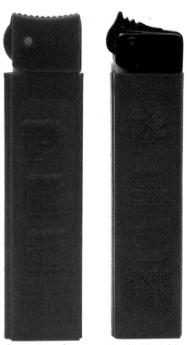

Newer regulars with matching inner sleeves. These are known as "mono regulars." (From the Johann Patek collection)

Rare long gray regular and "Klick and Spend" ad regular. These date to the early '70s. (From the Johann Patek collection)

Comparison of a new regular (on the left), and a vintage regular (on the right).

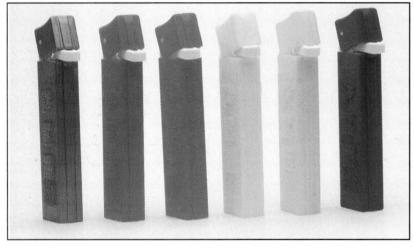

Current line of new U.S. regulars. First issued in the mid-1990s, they can still be found at retail.

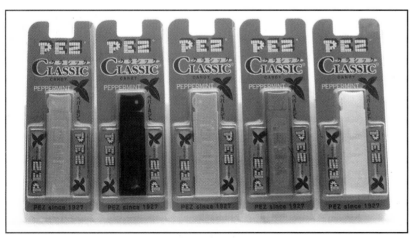

Current line of new regulars found only in Japan. Gold is the most difficult to find followed by black. The other three seem to be more common.

New Regulars

Mid-1990s

A new line of Regulars were produced in the 1990s, but with a noticeable difference in the cap. There is also a new line of Regulars with different colors that are only available in Japan.

New U.S. Regulars:	**$3-$5**
Monocromatic:	**$20-$25**
New Japan Regulars	
Pink, White, or Gray:	**$5-$10**
Gold:	**$30-$40**
Black:	**$15-$20**

Silver Glow, these were done in 1991 to commemorate the opening of a new PEZ® plant in Hungary.

Silver Glow, from the early 1990s.

Silver Glow
Early 1990s
Value: $25-$40

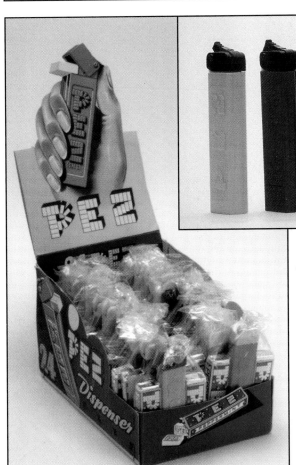

Vintage regulars can be found with many different cap and stem color combinations. The green dispenser on the far right is known as a "semi-transparent" because you can see the inner workings through the stem.

WOW! A complete box full of vintage regulars! (Note: the early style twist tops on the cello bags.) (From the Johann Patek collection)

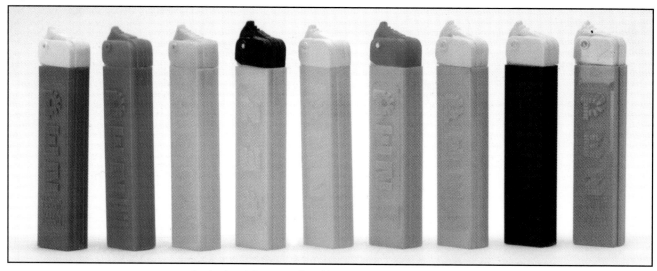

A selection of vintage regulars. (From the Johann Patek collection)

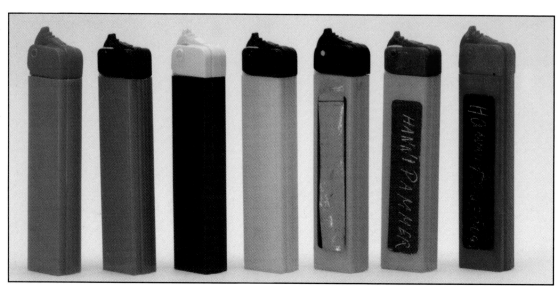

More vintage regulars with "personalized" variations. (From the Johann Patek collection)

A collection of disposable regulars. These dispensers have blank sides, came pre-filled with candy, and once emptied, could not be refilled. (From the Johann Patek collection)

Vintage Regulars
1950s
There are many different cap/stem color combinations including some that are semi-transparent through which you can see the inner workings of the dispenser.
Value: **$100-$150**

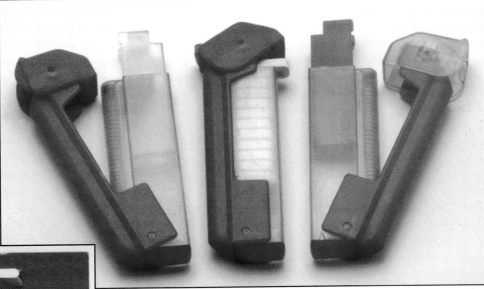

WOW! The ultra rare dispenser known as the "folding regular" or "super regular." They never went into production and few are known to exist. One sold on eBay in 2002 for $4500! (From the Johann Patek collection)

Vintage regular on card. Translation on card—
"Fill me with PEZ® and play with me."

Witch Regular

Mid-1950s

This is among the rarest of PEZ® dispensers. A picture of a witch is screened on both sides of the stem.

Value: **$3500+**

Witch regulars. Light and dark orange variations. The same picture of the witch is screened on both side of the stem. (From the Johann Patek collection)

European factory workers in the early 1950s at a table full of regulars and robots.

CHAPTER 12

Superheroes

Batman with Cape, from the late 1960s.

Batman, first appeared in the late 1960s and is still produced today. From left to right, original, with feet, black (available for a very short time in the mid-1990s), pointy ear version of the Dark Knight, and current Dark Knight version.

Rare Green Batman test mold. (From the Johann Patek collection)

Batman

Late 1960s, No Feet and With Feet

Batman has gone through several different looks and can still be found today. Batman with Cape is the earliest version and collectors should be aware that reproductions of the cape have been made. The original cape is somewhat translucent whereas reproduction capes are much thicker.

Batman with Cape:	**$75-$120**
Short Ears, No Feet:	**$20-$30**
Short Ears, With Feet:	**$10-$15**
Short Ears, With Feet, Black (available for a very short time in the mid-1990s):	**$10-$15**
Pointy Ear Dark Knight:	**$3-$6**
Rounded Ear Dark Knight (Current):	**$1-$2**

Captain America

Late 1970s, No Feet

Captain America was produced with a black and a blue mask—the black mask is tougher to find.

Black Mask:	**$100-$125**
Blue Mask:	**$85-$110**

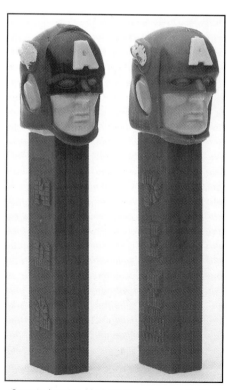

Captain America, black-mask version on left; blue-mask version on right.

S U P E R H E R O E S

Green Hornet variations. (From the Johann Patek collection)

Green Hornet Version A with smaller hat.

Green Hornet Version B with larger hat.

Green Hornet

Late 1960s, No Feet

The Green Hornet was produced in two different versions—one with a small hat and the other with a larger hat. The hat can be found in either brown or gray.

Version A (smaller hat): $200-$225
Version B (larger hat): $175-$200

Close-up of the Green Hornet head.

Rare, white eye version of the Incredible Hulk. (From the Johann Patek collection)

Incredible Hulk. (L to R) Dark green, light green, light green with feet.

One of a kind writing on the bottom sleeve of the white eyed Hulk, "endgultiges Muster E 19.5.78." Translation: "Final Sample May 19 1978." (From the Johann Patek collection)

Current version of the Incredible Hulk released in 1999.

Incredible Hulk

Late 1970s, No Feet and With Feet
The Incredible Hulk dispenser has been produced in varying shades of green.

Dark Green, No Feet:	**$40-$50**
Light Green, No Feet:	**$45-$55**
Light Green, With Feet:	**$3-$5**
With Teeth (current version, released 1999):	**$1-$2**

Softhead Superheroes

Late 1970s, No Feet
The heads on these dispensers are made of a soft eraser-like material and usually found only on USA marked stems. These are very popular with collectors. Characters in the series include: Batman, Penguin, Wonder Woman, Joker, and Batgirl.
Value: $150-$200 each

Softhead Superheroes. (L to R) Batman, Penguin, Wonder Woman, Joker, and Batgirl.

2000 Spider-Man. This version has a much bigger head than previous examples and is featured on a plain but unique card found only in Australia. $1-$3.

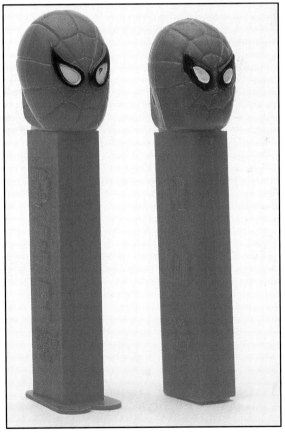

Spider-Man, first appeared in the late 1970s.

Spider-Man

Late 1970s, No Feet and With Feet
Several versions of Spider-Man have been produced.

Smaller Head, No Feet:	**$15-$20**
Medium Size Head, With Feet:	**$5-$8**
Larger Head, With Feet (Current):	**$1-$2**

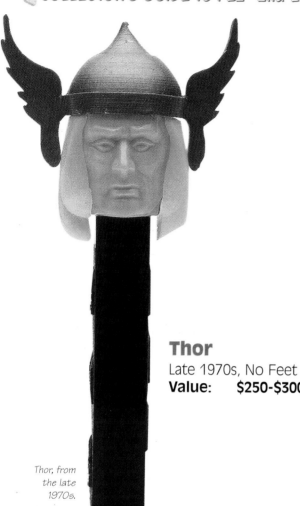

Thor

Late 1970s, No Feet
Value: **$250-$300**

*Thor, from
the late
1970s.*

*Wolverine, from
the X-Men comic.*

Wolverine

1999, With Feet
This is one of the characters from the popular
X-Men comic.
Value: $1-$2

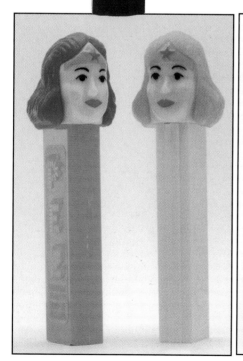

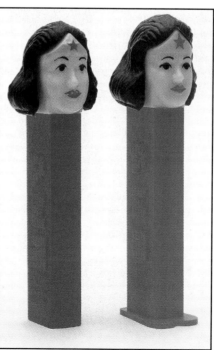

Wonder Woman

Late 1970s, No Feet and With
Feet
Two versions of Wonder
Woman were produced—the
earlier has a raised star on her
headband while on the
second version the star is flat.
**Raised Star,
 No Feet:** $20-$25
**Raised Star,
 With Feet:** $5-$10
**Flat Star,
 With Feet (Current):**
  $1-$2

*Unusual Wonder Woman test molds. (From the
Johann Patek collection)*

*Wonder Woman, first released late 1970s. The
dispenser on the left is the raised star version.*

Trucks

Various A-series trucks. (From the Johann Patek collection)

A-Series Truck

Late 1970s
The A-Series Trucks have four wheels and a single fender.
Value: $125-$150

A-Series truck. (From the Maryann Kennedy collection)

Various B-series trucks. (From the Johann Patek collection)

B-Series truck.

B-Series truck in rare olive green. (From the Maryann Kennedy collection)

B-Series Truck

Late 1970s
The B-Series Trucks have six wheels that move and a fender with a dip between the rear set of wheels.
Value: $60-$85   **Army Green (unusual color):** $200-$250

105

C-Series truck.

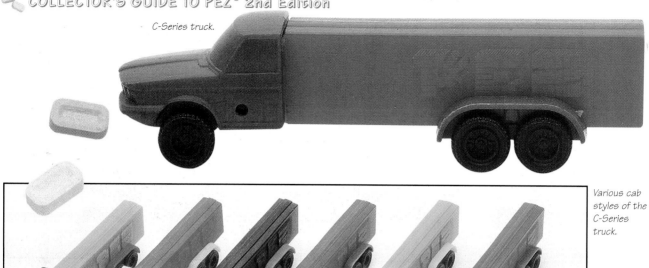

Various cab styles of the C-Series truck.

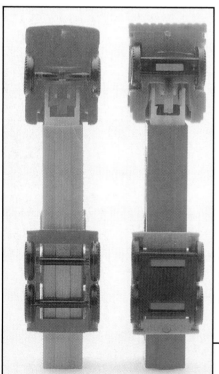

Comparison of the undersides of the C- and D-Series. The C-Series (left) has moveable wheels; the wheels on the D-Series (right) do not move.

C-Series Truck

Early 1980s

The C-Series Trucks have six wheels that move and a smooth fender over the rear set of wheels. Several cab styles were used on these trucks.

Value: $20-$30

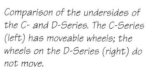

D-Series truck.

The trailers really glow in the dark!

D-Series Truck

Early 1990s-Current
The D-Series Trucks have six wheels and a smooth fender but, as of 1991, the wheels no longer move.

Value: $1-$2

Glow-in-the-Dark
  Version: $8-$12

D-Series trucks with glow-in-the-dark trailers.

Promotional toy truck. "Naschen & Spielen." Translation: "Eat and Play."

Promotional Truck

Approximately 8 inches long, these were produced in very small quantity and given to European food chains in 2001-2002.

Value: $40-$50

CHAPTER 14

Whistles

The Whistles are also known as Merry Music Makers.
PEZ® began producing these musical dispensers in the early 1980s.

A group of Merry Music Makers. (L to R) Dog, Camel, Koala, Rooster, Monkey.

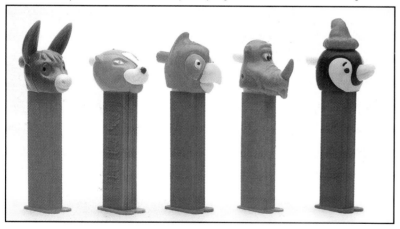

More Merry Music Makers. (L to R) Donkey, Tiger, Parrot, Rhino, Penguin.

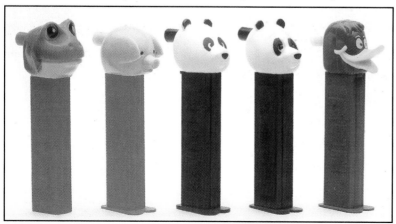

(L to R) Frog, Pig, Panda (stencil eyes), Panda (removable eyes), Duck.

Camel
No Feet and With Feet
The camel can be found with either a brown or a tan head.
No Feet: $60-$75
With Feet: $40-$60

Clown
No Feet and With Feet
No Feet: $12-$15
With Feet: $5-$10

Dog
No Feet and With Feet
No Feet: $30-$40
With Feet: $20-$30

Donkey
No Feet and With Feet
No Feet: $12-$15
With Feet: $5-$10

Duck
No Feet and With Feet
No Feet: $45-$55
With Feet: $30-$40

Frog
No Feet and With Feet
No Feet: $40-$50
With Feet: $30-$40

Indian
With Feet
Value: $25-$35

Koala
No Feet and With Feet
No Feet: $35-$45
With Feet: $15-$25

Lamb
No Feet and With Feet
No Feet: $25-$35
With Feet: $15-$25

Monkey
No Feet and With Feet
No Feet: $30-$40
With Feet: $25-$30

Owl
With Feet
The Owl is very rare and only a few are known to exist.
Value: $2000+

Panda
No Feet and With Feet
The Panda was made with removable eyes and with stencil eyes.
Removable Eyes, No Feet: $25-$35
Removable Eyes, With Feet: $20-$25
Stencil Eyes, With Feet: $5-$10

Clown whistle.

Owl whistle – this is a very rare dispenser. (From the Maryann Kennedy collection)

Lamb whistle.

Two views of the Indian whistle.

Parrot

No Feet and With Feet
A rare variation of the Parrot exists with a yellow head and a red beak; more common versions have a red head with a yellow beak.

No Feet:	**$15-$20**
With Feet:	**$5-$10**
Yellow Head, Red Beak:	**$300+**

Rare version of the Parrot whistle with red beak. (From the Maryann Kennedy collection)

Penguin

With Feet

Value:	**$5-$10**

Pig

No Feet and With Feet

No Feet:	**$50-$60**
With Feet:	**$35-$45**

Rhino

No Feet and With Feet

No Feet:	**$15-$25**
With Feet:	**$5-$10**

Rooster

No Feet and With Feet

No Feet:	**$35-$45**
With Feet:	**$25-$35**

Tiger

With Feet

Value:	**$5-$10**

Coach's Whistle

No Feet and With Feet

No Feet:	**$35-$50**
With Feet:	**$1-$3**

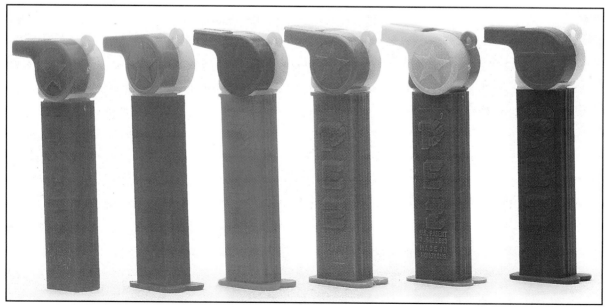

An assortment of the Coach's Whistle.

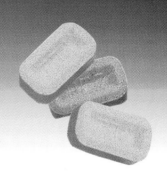

CHAPTER 15

Sports

The newest trend in PEZ® collecting is sports team dispensers. The Chicago Cubs were the first to have a "PEZ® dispenser day" at Wrigley Field in June of 2000. The first 15,000 fans through the gate received a limited edition Charlie Brown dispenser with a commemorative souvenir card. Other teams took notice of the Cubs' huge success and started their own "PEZ® day" at the ball park. This trend is not limited to just major league baseball, teams such as the Orlando Magic and Washington Wizards (basketball) and Philadelphia Kixx (soccer) have also followed suit.

With the wide variety of sports and sports teams, the possibilities are almost limitless. Initial offerings of these dispensers on Internet auction sites have seen prices in the $50 range for one dispenser! Once eager collectors snap up an example for their collection, prices have seemed to drop back but hold steady in the $20-$30 range. Most of these events give away 15,000 dispensers, a very small quantity in relation to the number PEZ® makes of a character sold at the retail level. Given that, and the fact these events are held for one day in different parts of the country, I think these special dispensers will continue to hold a higher value, not only with PEZ® collectors but with sports memorabilia collectors as well.

**Cubs/Charlie Brown Pez®
Dispenser Day**
Exclusive Limited Edition!

Wednesday, June 14, at 1:20
Chicago Cubs vs. New York Mets
at Wrigley Field

sponsored by

www.cubs.com

Cubs Charlie Brown w/card: $25-$35.

Dispensers and teams to date:

June 14, 2000 Cubs Charlie Brown with logo on cap
June 26, 2001 Cubs Joe Cool with logo on baseball cap
July 8, 2001 Minnesota Twins T.C. Bear
September 15, 2001 Chicago Cubs Homer Simpson with sticker on bag
September 23, 2001 Philadelphia Phillies baseball with team logo
November 9, 2001 Orlando Magic basketball with team logo
February 3, 2002 Washington Wizards basketball with team logo
March 2 & 3, 2002 Philadelphia Kixx white ball with team logo (only
    2500 were given out each day)
March 15, 2002 New Jersey Nets basketball with team logo
June 27, 2002 Chicago Cubs baseball with team logo
June 28, 2002 Columbus Clippers baseball with team logo
July 5, 2002 New York Yankees baseball with team logo
July 14, 2002 Minnesota Twins baseball with team logo
August 2, 2002 Washington Mystics (WNBA) white basketball with
    team logo
August 28, 2002 Staten Island Yankees baseball
September 14, 2002 Arizona Diamondbacks baseball with team logo
October 30, 2002 Seattle Supersonics basketball

Chicago Cubs Joe Cool, $20-$30. Minnesota Twins T.C. Bear, $10-$20. Philadelphia Kixx soccer ball, $25-$35. Washington Wizards basketball, $25-$35. New Jersey Nets basketball, $25-$35.

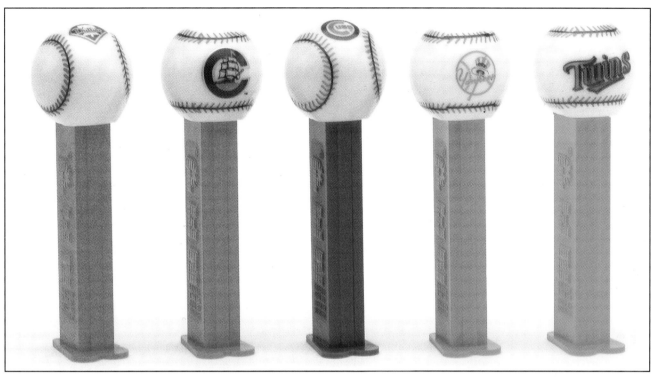

Philadelphia Phillies, $20-$30. Columbus Clippers, $15-$25. Chicago Cubs, $20-$30. New York Yankees, $25-$35. Minnesota Twins, $10-$20.

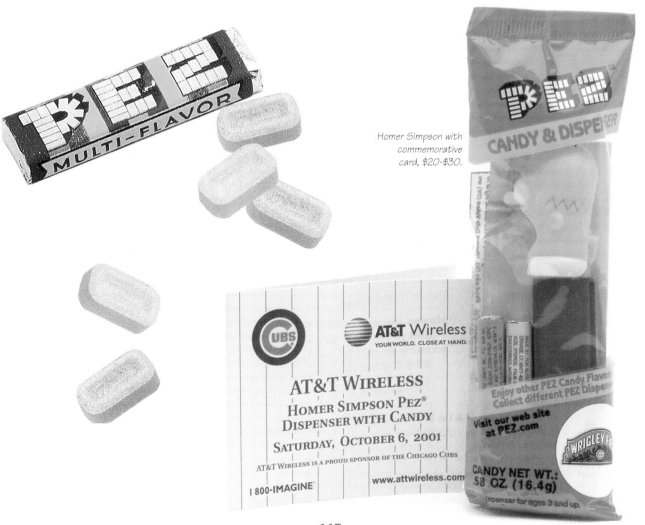

Homer Simpson with commemorative card, $20-$30.

CHAPTER 16

Miscellaneous Dispensers

Baseball set, from the mid-1960s. This is difficult to find with the bat and home plate. The vending box is also very rare, only a few examples are known to have survived. (From the Maryann Kennedy collection)

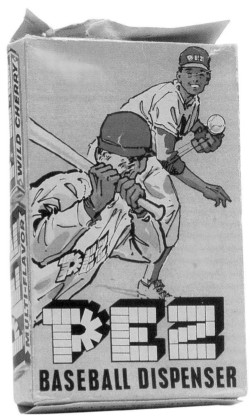

The backside of the baseball vending box.

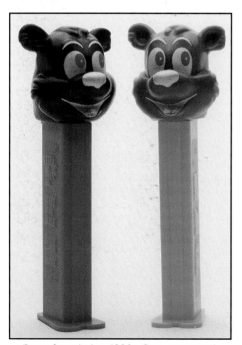

Bears, from the late 1990s. These are unusual color variations.

Baseball Set
Mid 1960s, No Feet
This set consisted of a dispenser with a baseball mitt "head" and a removable ball, bat, and home plate. It is difficult to find with the bat and home plate. The vending box is also very rare as only a few examples are known to have survived.
Value: **$600-$800**

Bear
Late 1990s, With Feet
This dispenser uses the same head as the Icee Bear and the FAO Schwarz Bear and is not available in the U.S.
Value: **$5-$10**

Bubbleman, only available from PEZ® mail-in offer. This is the first set offered. They have the copyright date of 1992 on the dispenser but didn't appear until the fall of 1996.

Neon Bubbleman, set of 5 available from PEZ® mail-in offer. First appeared in 1998 with the matching neon color hat and stem.

Bubbleman

Mid-1990s, With Feet

This dispenser was only available from PEZ® through a mail-in offer. The Bubbleman was the first set offered in this manner. They have the copyright date of 1992 on the dispenser but didn't appear until the fall of 1996.

Value Originals:	**$5-$10 each**
Neon Bubbleman (1998):	**$3-$6 each**
Crystal Bubbleman (1999):	**$3-$6 each**
Glowing Bubbleman:	**$3-$6 each**

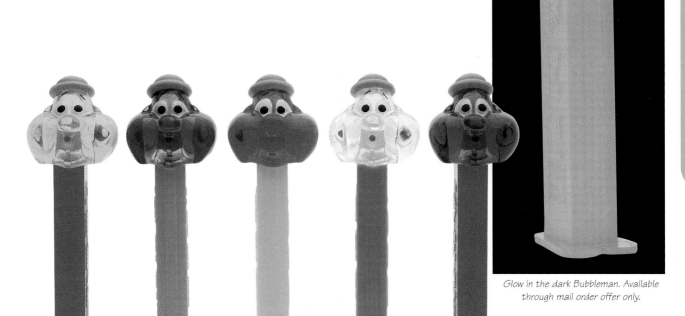

Glow in the dark Bubbleman. Available through mail order offer only.

Crystal Bubbleman, set of 5 available from PEZ® mail-in offer. First appeared summer of 1999.

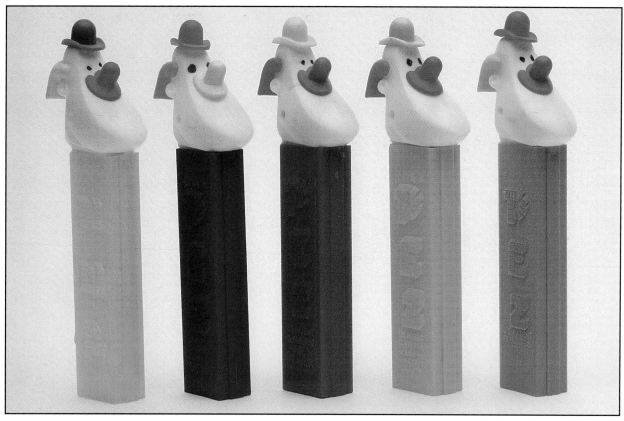

Long face clown or clown with chin, from the mid-1970s.

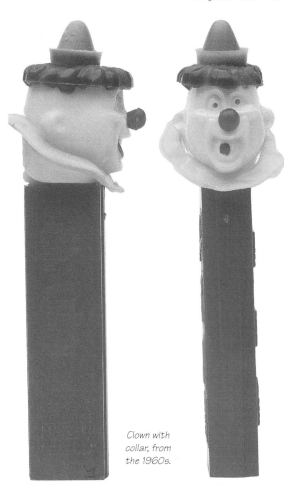

Clown with collar, from the 1960s.

Clown with Chin
(Also known as Long Face Clown)
Mid-1970s, No Feet
This dispenser can be found with many hair, hat, and nose color combinations.
Value: $85-$100

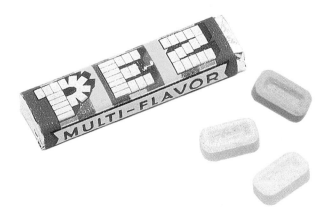

Clown with Collar
1960s, No Feet
Value: $60-$75

5MISCELLANEOUS DISPENSERS

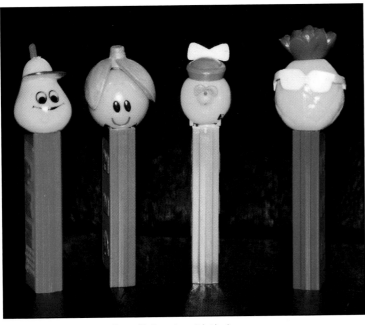

Crazy Fruit series with the Lemon.

Crazy Fruit series. (L to R) Pear, Orange, and Pineapple.
(Pear and Pineapple from the Maryann Kennedy collection)

Crazy Fruit Series

Mid-1970s, No Feet

The Orange first appeared in the mid-1970s, followed by the Pear and Pineapple in the late 1970s. The Pineapple is the hardest of the three to find, followed by the Pear then the Orange. The Lemon was made as production sample but never produced.

Orange:	**$200-$250**
Pear:	**$800-$1000**
Pineapple:	**$2500-$3000**
Lemon:	**$3000+**

The ultra-rare Lemon Crazy Fruit dispenser – this is a production sample; the dispenser was never produced. (From the Dora Dwyer collection)

Ultra-rare short stem pineapple on the left and regular version on the right. Notice the sticker on the stem, it says "Ananas-Hong/Kong.nicht/genehmigte Aus/fuhrung.26.6.78." Translation: "Pineapple Hong Kong not accepted variation 06-26-78."
(From the Johann Patek collection)

M I S C E L L A N E O U S   D I S P E N S E R S

117

New crystal ball dispensers.

Crystal Ball Dispenser
Sold through a 2002 mail-in offer for $15.95. It has tiny silver sparkles in the stem and base. The first 2500 were made by mistake using silver stars, the remaining production will have blue stars.

Value: $15.95

Die-cuts from the early 1960s. (L to R) Casper, Donald Duck, Mickey Mouse, Easter Rabbit, Bozo.

Die-Cuts
Early 1960s

A Die-Cut dispenser is one in which a design is cut into the side of the stem. The cut-out usually reveals an inner sleeve of a different color. Several dispensers were made with a die-cut stem in the 1960s.

Casper:	$250-$275
Donald Duck:	$175-$200
Mickey Mouse:	$125-$175
Easter Rabbit:	$500-$600
Bozo:	$175-$200

eBay Dispensers

eBay crystal heart dispensers, available on-line from the eBay store in 2000, this set of 4 dispensers was available for $10 per set. Limited to 5000 sets they quickly sold out. eBay also presented their employees with a variation of this dispenser. It has a black base, glow in the dark heart with black eBay logo.

Crystal set: **$40-$60**
Employee
  dispenser: **$75-$100**

eBay hearts.

FAO Schwarz Bear—sold only in FAO Schwarz toy stores in 1999.

FAO Schwarz Bear

1999, With Feet
This dispenser was sold only in FAO Schwarz toy stores. This bear first appeared in late August of 1999 and had a retail price of $3.99.

Value: **$4-$5**

Fuzzy Friends

First released in 2000 each bear has a name, birthdate, and hometown. Each bear has "PEZ" embroidered down the side of the stem, a backpack clip, and articulated arms and legs. A new series released in 2002 called "Wild Zoo" has 5 similar animal dispensers.

Fuzzy Friends: **$4-$6 each**
Wild Zoo: **$4-$6 each**

Fuzzy Friends (L to R) Purple bear is Gilbert, Black and White bear is Jade, Orange bear is T.J., and the Brown bear is Buddy.

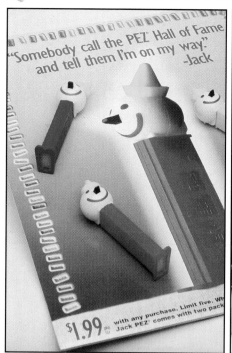

Jack in the Box dispenser on 1999 promotional poster.

2000 Jack in the Box promotion. This is the same dispenser used in the 1999 promotion but now with a price of only 99 cents.

Jack in the Box

1999, With Feet
This is a restaurant promotion done in the likeness of the Jack in the Box mascot "Jack." It appeared for a very limited time in June of 1999. Jack in the Box, found mostly in western states, allowed customers to buy these with an additional food purchase for $1.99. Three different stem colors: red, blue, and yellow.

Value: **$10 each**

Magic PEZ® dispenser.

Jungle Mission Survival Kit.

Jungle Mission

Everything you will need the next time you're lost in the jungle! A flashlight, ruler, compass, backpack clip, magnifying glass and most important—a PEZ® dispenser! Can be found in several different color combinations.

Value: **$3-$6 each**

Magic PEZ® Dispenser

Dispenses candy from the hat and has an additional compartment on the bottom that holds an extra pack of candy that you can make disappear then magically re-appear! Can be found in many different color combinations.

Value: **$3-$6 each**

A trio of Make-a-Faces! (From the Johann Patek collection)

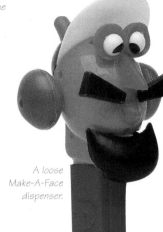

A loose Make-A-Face dispenser.

Front of U.S. card. (From the Johann Patek collection)

MISCELLANEOUS DISPENSERS

Make-a-Face

Early 1970s, No Feet

This dispenser first appeared in 1972 but was quickly discontinued as it had too many tiny pieces that could be easily removed and swallowed by a child. Also, the dispenser was poorly packaged—the bubble frequently came loose from the card spilling the parts, and rendering it unsaleable. It is rumored what stock was left of these after they were discontinued was ground up, re-melted and used to mold the headdress for the Indian Chief. The U.S. version contained 17 separate pieces and the European 16, not counting the shoes. This is a very difficult dispenser to find still intact on the card.

U.S. version m.o.c.:
$3000+
European version m.o.c.:
$2500+

Back of U.S. card. (From the Johann Patek collection)

Front of European card. (From the Johann Patek collection)

Back of European card. (From the Johann Patek collection)

Mr. Mystic

No Feet

Some doubt the authenticity of this piece, citing it as nothing more than the head of Zorro with a ringmaster hat on it. Currently there is documentation from PEZ® International that states his existence.

Value: $500+

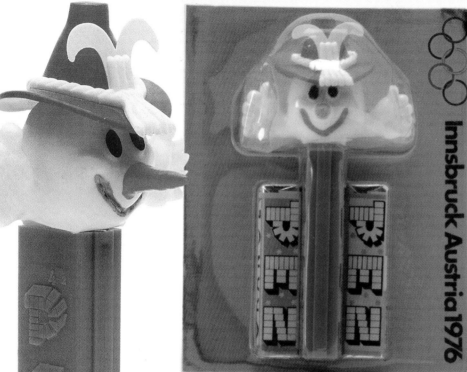

The mysterious Mr. Mystic. (From the Maryann Kennedy collection)

Olympic Snowman still on the card! (From the Johann Patek collection)

Long-nose version of the Olympic Snowman from the 1976 Winter Olympics in Innsbruck, Austria. (From the Maryann Kennedy collection)

Olympic Snowman

No Feet

This dispenser was made for the 1976 winter Olympics in Innsbruck, Austria. A very hard to find dispenser, it can also be found in a "short nose" version.

Value: $500-$600

A paper advertisement showing the Olympic Snowman valued at $50+. (From the Maryann Kennedy collection)

Vucko, the Olympic Wolf from the 1984 Sarajevo Olympics. Shown here with a paper insert. (From the Maryann Kennedy collection)

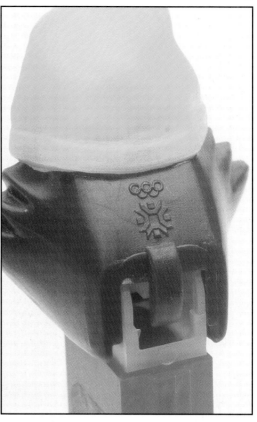

Both the Olympic symbol and Olympic rings appear on the back of Vucko's head.

Vucko variations; without hat, with hat, and with bobsled helmet. (From the Maryann Kennedy collection)

Olympic Wolves (also called Vucko (voo sh-co) wolves)

With Feet

This very hard to find dispenser was made for the 1984 Olympic games in Sarajevo, Yugoslavia. Variations exist without hat, with hat, and with bobsled helmet.

Wolf, no hat:	$350-$450
Wolf, no hat, unusual brown nose:	$375-$425
Wolf with hat:	$450-$550
Wolf with bobsled helmet:	$500-$600

PIF the Dog

With Feet
PIF was offered as a premium in a German "YPS" comic in 1989.
If you look closely you can see his name PIF on his left ear.
Value: $85-$100

PIF the Dog – a German comic character.

Easter Playworld set.

Christmas Playworld set.

Shell Gas Playworld set.

Playworld Sets

Early 1990s, With Feet, Non-U.S.
These sets featured a single dispenser along with a matching body part. The sets usually have a theme such as Easter or Christmas. After opening the package, the cardboard piece inserted with it would unfold into three sections. It contained related scenery which could serve as a backdrop in which to play with the dispenser.

Easter set: $20-$25
Christmas set: $10-$15
Shell Gas set: $20-$25

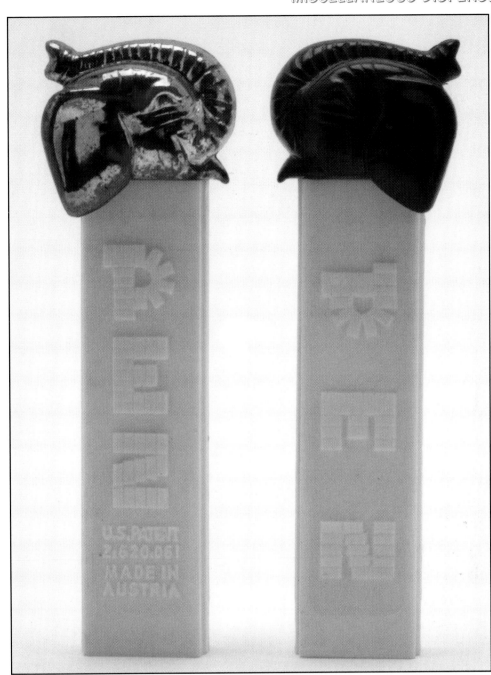

Very rare variations of the political elephant. (From the Johann Patek collection)

Political Elephant

No Feet

This is an extremely rare dispenser, only a few are known to exist. It is thought to represent the elephant of the Republican political party. In early 1997 an old file was discovered in the PEZ® factory in Connecticut containing a press release and an old photo of a special set of dispensers. The press release was dated June 13, 1961 and had the heading "President Kennedy receives PEZ® souvenirs on his visit to Vienna." It went on to detail the set and then said "To the President of the United States of America J.F. Kennedy with the Compliments of PEZ®." The set contained in a wooden, cigar like box had three dispensers; a Donkey for the President (to represent the Democratic Party), a Golden Glow for Jackie, a Bozo die-cut for Caroline, and three packs of candy for each. To date, neither the Donkey nor the complete set have surfaced. The elephant as pictured has a shiny, golden colored head with his trunk extending over the top of his head.

Value: $6000+

Psychedelic Flower

Late 1960s, No Feet

Very much a product of their time, these dispensers came packaged with flower flavor candy. They can be found with several different stickers including, "mod pez," "go-go pez," and different "luv pez" versions on at least one side. The side that has the sticker will be completely smooth. Some dispensers had stickers on both sides and are considered to be worth a bit more than a one-sticker dispenser. A collector's edition remake was produced in the late 1990s and was available from PEZ® through a mail-in offer. The remake versions have the raised PEZ® logo on the stem and do not have stickers on either side. They are also marked with a copyright symbol and 1967—the originals do not have a date on them.

Original: $450-$550
Remake, m.o.c.: $15-$20

Psychedelic Flower from the late 1960s.

Hard to find yellow and deep red flower variations. (From the Johann Patek collection)

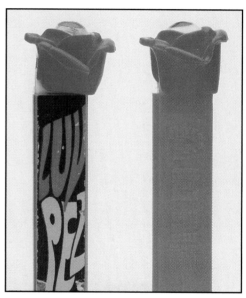

Comparison of a vintage Psychedelic Flower (left) and a Collector's Edition remake.

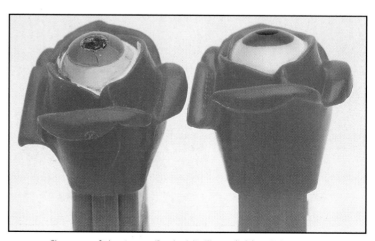

Collector's Edition Psychedelic Flower on card—these dispensers were available in 1999 through a mail-in offer.

Close-ups of the vintage Psychedelic Flower (left) and the remake.

Psychedelic Hand

Late 1960s, No Feet

The Hand also came packaged with flower flavor candy, and will have at least one sticker. The side that has the sticker will be completely smooth. Some dispensers had stickers on both sides and are considered to be worth a bit more than a one-sticker dispenser.

A collector's edition remake was produced in the late 1990s and was only available through a PEZ® mail-in offer. The remake versions have the raised PEZ® logo on the stem and do not have stickers on either side. They are also marked with a copyright symbol and 1967—the originals do not have a date on them.

Original:	**$350-$450**
Original, Black hand:	**$450-$550**
Remake, m.o.c.:	**$15-$20**

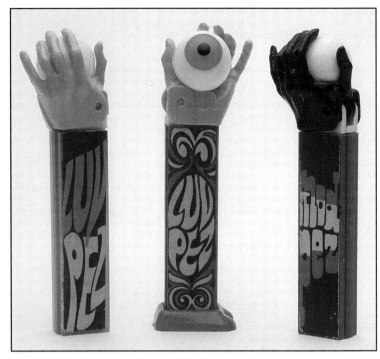

Psychedelic Hands from the late 1960s. The Black Hand on the right is a less common variation.

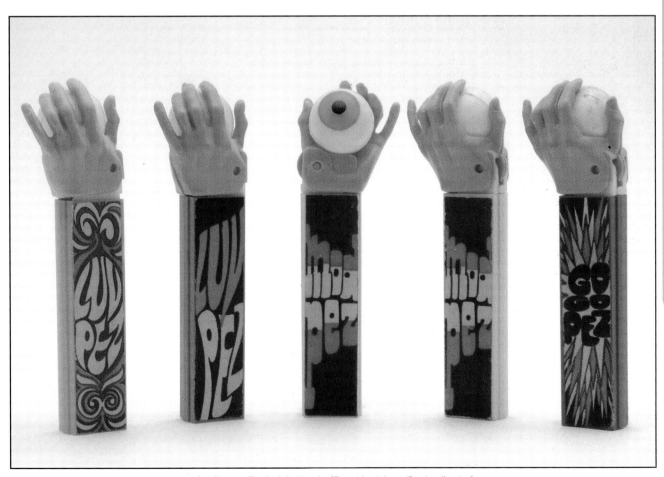

A collection Psychedelic Hands. (From the Johann Patek collection)

A collection of Black Psychedelic Hands. (From the Johann Patek collection)

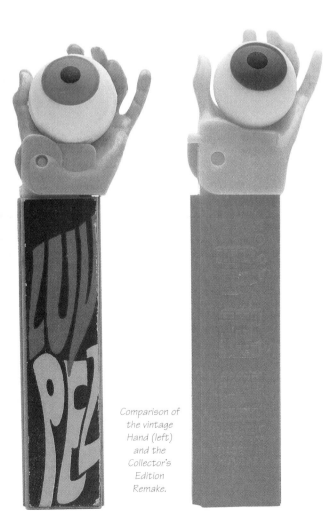

Comparison of the vintage Hand (left) and the Collector's Edition Remake.

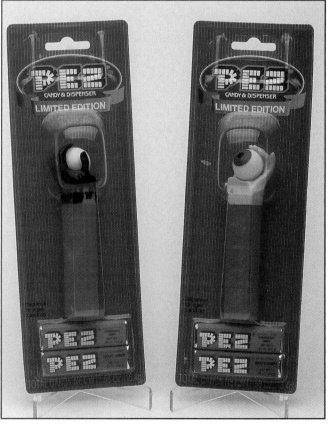

Collector's Edition Hand on card – offered by PEZ® in 1998 through a mail-in offer.

2001 Limited Edition Crystal Psychedelic Hands.

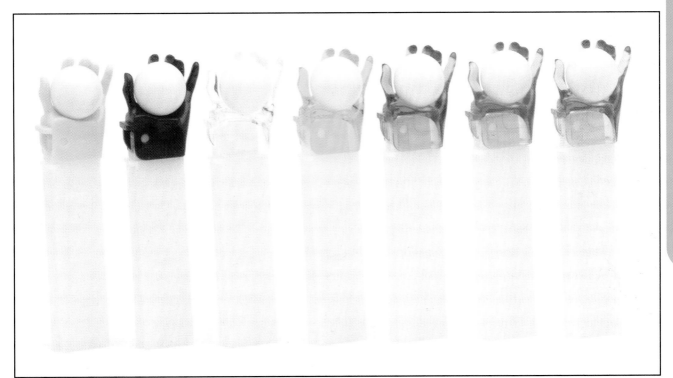

Test pieces from the late 1990s.

*Very rare gold robot.
(From the Johann
Patek collection)*

Robot
(Also known as the Spacetrooper)
1950s

This is one of the few "full body" dispensers. They stand approximately 3 1/2" tall and have the letters "PEZ" on their back. They are tough to find.

Red or Blue:	**$350-$450**
Yellow or Dark Blue:	**$300-$400**
Shiny Gold (very rare):	**$2000+**

Assembling robots!

Robot or Spacetroopers from the late 1950s. A "full body" dispenser.

Back of blue robots.
(From the Johann Patek collection)

Sourz

Released summer of 2002. Pineapple, blue raspberry, watermelon, and green apple come with new sour PEZ® candy!
Value: $1-$2 each

Pucker up! It's the new Sourz!

Sparefroh

Early 1970s, No Feet

"Sparefroh" is German for "happy saver." October 31st of each year in Europe is World Savings Day when all people are encouraged to save money in a bank. (Thus the tie-in with the coin that is glued to the front of the stem) This was a gift to children who put money in their bank account on that day. There are two different stem inscriptions: "110 Jahre Allgemeine Sparkasse in Linz" and "Deine Sparkasse." The dispenser must have the coin attached to be considered complete.

Value: **$1200-$1500**

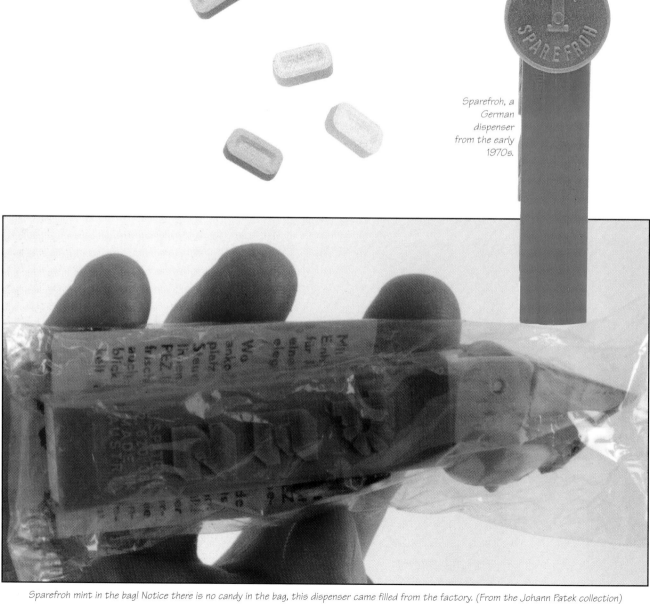

Sparefroh, a German dispenser from the early 1970s.

Sparefroh mint in the bag! Notice there is no candy in the bag, this dispenser came filled from the factory. (From the Johann Patek collection)

Smiley

Have a nice day! It's the smiley face dispenser, found only at Wal-Mart, this guy can be found on purple, green, orange, blue, hot pink, or yellow stems.
Value: **$1-$3**

USA Hearts

2002 mail-in offer. A set of 6 was offered for $8.95
Value: **$8.95**

Have a nice day!

USA heart.

Zielpunkt

1999, With Feet
Zielpunkt is a grocery chain in Austria. They commissioned PEZ® International to immortalize their mascot "Smiley" in a unique and likable dispenser. This dispenser is not available in the U.S.
Value: **$10-$15**

Zielpunkt, a grocery store chain in Austria, commissioned PEZ® International to produce a dispenser of their mascot "Smiley."

CHAPTER 17

Ad Sheets

Ad sheets were only distributed to people "in the business" — salesmen, brokers, dealers, etc. They were not meant for the general public, making them difficult to find. Some collectors pursue only the dispensers and have little interest in these sheets. Others enjoy collecting anything related to PEZ®.

You can learn a lot by studying ad sheets — such as how dispensers were packaged, who distributed them, how much they cost and even unusual variations of a particular dispenser. Depending on the dispenser(s) pictured, size of the ad, and artwork, prices for these ad sheets can go from a couple of dollars for a current ad to a couple of hundred dollars for a vintage ad of a popular character(s) like the Universal Studios movie monsters.

Universal Monster ad sheet from the 1960s. Front and back pictured. $200+.

Snow White ad sheet from the 1960s. $50+.

Holiday advertisements with animated Santa and Snowman and an ad from 1979 with Disney characters. It seems a large variety of these ads were done from the early '70s to the early '80s in Croatia. They are printed on cheap paper similar to newspaper. Many different ads can be found in on-line auctions for a reasonable price. Most ads $10-$15 each

German ad sheet from the 1970s. Notice the doctor does not have hair: $15-$20.

German ad sheet from the 1970s. $15-$20.

Batman ad sheet from around 1965. $100+.

Muppets sales sheet from 1991. If you look closely you will notice the dispensers pictured are prototypes and not actual production pieces. In order to promote an upcoming line before it comes out, many times production pieces are not available in time to use with the advertising. $3-$5.

Back of the Batman ad sheet.

Going back to its roots by promoting an adult breath mint, the remake of the PEZ® regular. 1990s. $2-$4.

PEZ® Pal ad sheet from the 1970s. If you look closely notice the Engineer, Stewardess, Pilot, and Sheriff all appear to be prototypes and not actual production pieces. $40+.

PEZ® ad sheet from the 1960s. $50+.

Spinner rack ad sheet from the 1970s. $30+.

PEZ® Pal ad sheet from the 1970s. $40+.

Pezi ad sheet from the 1960s. $40+.

1970s floor shipper ad sheet. $25-$35.

Superheroes ad sheet. $30-$40.

Candy brochure from the 1990s showing the PEZ® factory in Orange, Connecticut. $4-$8.

Reverse of the psychedelic ad sheet.

Make-a-Face and Olympic Wolf advertisements from a Croatian magazine. This is the only ad for a Make-a-Face I have ever seen. $20-$35 each.

CHAPTER 18

Candy Packs

While the candy itself has always been at the core of the business, collecting the individual candy packs has only recently begun to gain interest among a small group of PEZ® collectors. The desire to find odd and unusual candy packs has piqued some collector's interest, causing prices to rise into the hundred-dollar range for some rare packs. Examples of rare candy packs include those that have pictures of a regular on the back, small sample packs from a tradeshow that only contained three or four pieces of candy, or simply a flavor that did not sell well such as flower flavor from the 1960s. These kinds of packs are very difficult to find and therefore command higher prices.

Condition, flavor, and language are the three most important factors when determining the value of a candy pack. Age also plays a part—generally the older the pack the higher the price. The ingredient list on the side also plays a part but should be considered more of a variation than a value factor.

In the late 1990s European candy packs were modified and manufactured with the label printed right on the foil. Currently, these have little value beyond retail price. Earlier packs that have a paper label separate from the foil will be more desirable as candy pack collecting gains interest. Prices for candy packs can vary widely as they are just beginning to be collected.

Known PEZ® flavors include: Assorted Fruit, Grape, Lemon, Orange, Strawberry, Peppermint, Cherry, Chocolate, Anise, Chlorophyll, Coffee, Eucalyptus, Flower Flavor, Hot Cinnamon, IZO (vitamins), Licorice, Lime, Menthol, and Wild Cherry. The new sour flavors include: Green Apple, Pineapple, Blue Raspberry, and Watermelon. Many of the less popular flavors, such as flower and chlorophyll, were quickly discontinued making the candy packs quite scarce. Some flavors are only available in Europe.

Examples of various cherry-flavored candy packs. Some are rather tough to find such as the twin packs from the 1970s. $1-$20+.

Peppermint refills. Some are hard to find such as the Super Mint and the small sample pack on the right. $1-$20+.

Strawberry refills. The "Erdbeer" (German for strawberry) and long pack in the back can be tough to find. $1-$15+.

Various candy packs. The two on the right offering a mail in premium are tough to find. $1-20+.

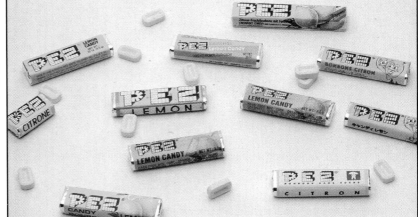

Lemon refills. The small sample pack on the left is hard to find. $1-$20+.

Grape refills. The Golden grape is especially tough to find. $1-$20+.

Various multi flavor packs. The one marked "Pez USA" was not intended for U.S. sales, instead it was sold in eastern Europe in the late 1990s and advertised as a piece of "Americana." (Also notice the Kosher pack, middle right) $1-$15.

Orange refills. $1-$20+.

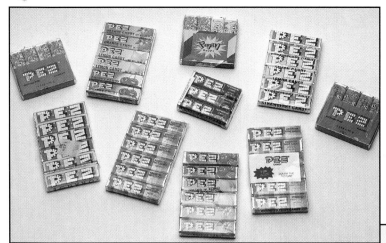

Various multi-pack refills. Notice the original price tag (bottom left) of 34¢!

Box candy from Europe. $4-$8 each.

Miscellaneous candy packs. (Clockwise from top) Choco: $20-$30; Lime: $20-$30; SIXO pack is quite rare: $75-$85; Red label Traubenzucker: $15-$20; Raspberry from Czech Republic: .50-$1; TAB pack (and Austrian game manufacturer): $20-$30; Luftansa pack is from the German airline commemorating a Y2K party held in Munich on 12-31-99; McDonald's pack was found only in Austria, shown both front and back: $3-$5; 2000 Cola: $1-$2.

Hard to find candy packs from the 1950s advertising the "Pez Box" dispenser on the back. $125-$175 each. (From the Johann Patek collection)

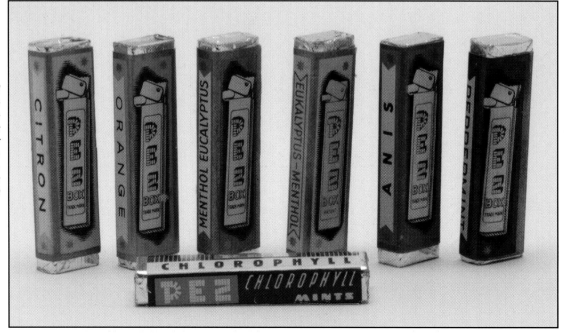

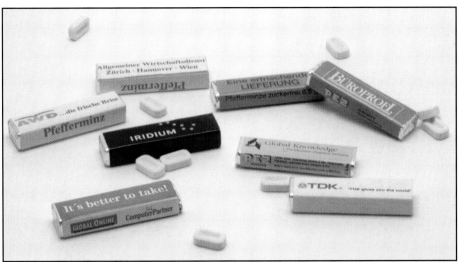

A variety of advertising candy packs. $3-$10 each. (From the Johann Patek collection)

Various candy packs, the Eukalyptus Menthol pack is very difficult to find. $100+

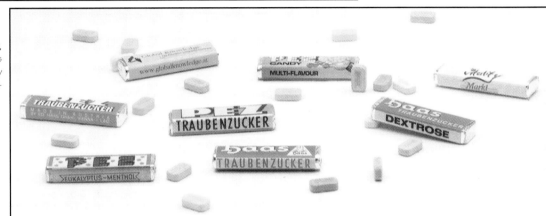

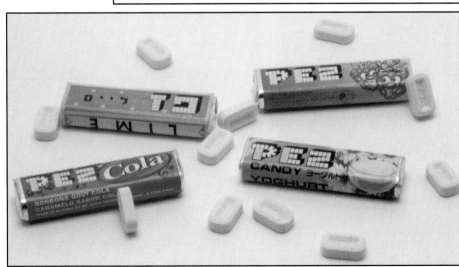

Some unusual variations and rare yoghurt pack. $10-$30+ each. (From the Johann Patek collection)

Selection of newer candy packs.

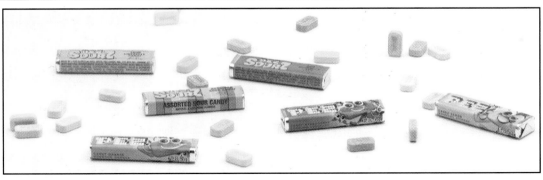

Candy sample pack from the 1950s. These were usually given away at candy conventions or trade shows. $150+. Translation "... and now ...". (From the Johann Patek collection)

Inside shot of sample pack.

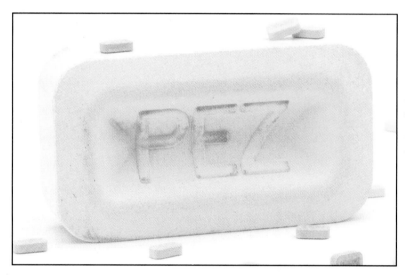

Giant piece of PEZ® candy! These are created as a gift at certain European factories for potential customers or visiting VIP's.

Candy pack ad sheet from the 1950s. (From the Johann Patek collection)

PEZ drops from the mid-1920s! (From the Nick Petracca collection)

Porcelain metal advertising sign. Probably from the mid to late 1950s. (From the Silvia Biermayr/Gerhard Trebbin collection)

Supermint European advertising poster-probably late 1950s early 1960s. $200+ (From the Silvia Biermayr/Gerhard Trebbin collection)

Early 1950s. Notice the great selection of candy refill boxes!

Chapter 19

Counter Boxes

Vintage counter boxes can be expensive and tough to find. As it was a disposable item, when the product was gone the shopkeeper threw it away and ordered another – it was never meant to be kept. Most boxes contained 24 or 36 dispensers, which in theory means there could only be one box for every two or three dozen dispensers that survived!

Pricing an old counter box depends on the condition, size, rarity, characters or theme depicted, and the artwork. Boxes, like ad sheets, inserts, and other paper related items are not popular with all collectors. Boxes that were produced for a specific group are much harder to find and usually bring more money than generic boxes. Most of these were produced in the early to mid 1960s and are called "single theme boxes" because they had one specific purpose. Single theme boxes include such characters as The Jungle Book, Popeye, and Green Hornet. Boxes showing a generic character allowed more flexibility in what was placed inside them and quickly became more common in the 1970s.

Old cigar type box full of peppermint refills dating from the late 1940s. $2000+. (From the Johann Patek collection)

A rare "six pak" refill box from the 1970s. Notice the Admiral on the side: $300+.

Reverse side of "six pak" box.

Single pack refill box from the 1970s. $200+.

Reverse side of single pack box.

Small single pack refill box with die-cut header. Dates to the 1950s. $350+. (From the Johann Patek collection)

Single pack refill boxes from the 1950s. These are very difficult to find and seldom turn up. $400-$600 each. (Notice the candy packs say "free sample"—these packs are extremely rare. $125-$175 each.)

Small acrylic box with blue embossed lid. This box dates to the 1950s. $200-$250+. (From the Johann Patek collection)

Three compartment acrylic candy refill display from the 1950s. Top compartment shows a hand dispensing candy from a BOX patent regular, the second shows how to set up the display and the third shows a single pack of peppermint candy. Display should have 2 small curved acrylic legs to be considered complete. The display box shows up occasionally but the legs are almost impossible to find. Display $250+; With legs $450+.

Full boxes of Cherry and Traubenzucker candy packs. $200+. (From the Johann Patek collection)

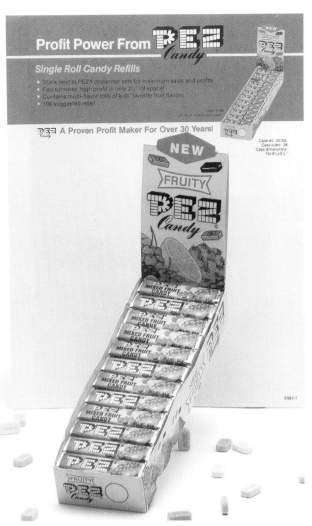

Fruit refill counter box from the 1970s with matching ad sheet. $250+.

Orange refills and box from the 1950s. Box: $75+;
Candy packs: $15-$20.

Orange refill box
from the 1980s:
$25-$35.

Peppermint refill counter
box from the late '90s.
$10-$15.

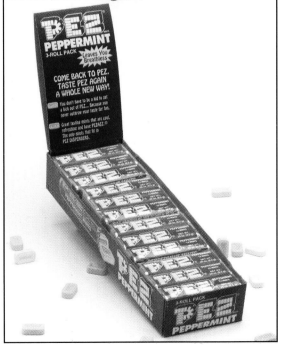

1960s "brick" of
Golden PEZ® refills:
$200+.

Cola candy box, and 8-pack refills. Refills: $6-$12.

Candy refill boxes from Europe. Early 1990s. $5-$10 each.

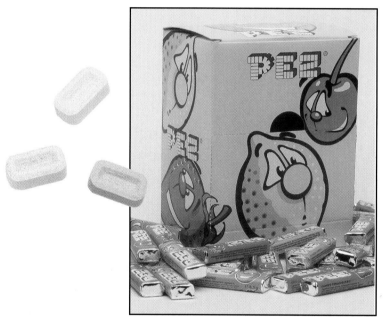

Canadian fruit flavor
refills with counter box.

1950s shipping carton that held two-dozen Peppermint refill boxes.
Items like this are very tough to come by but have little interest for
most collectors. $50+.

Disney counter box from the 1960s: $100+.

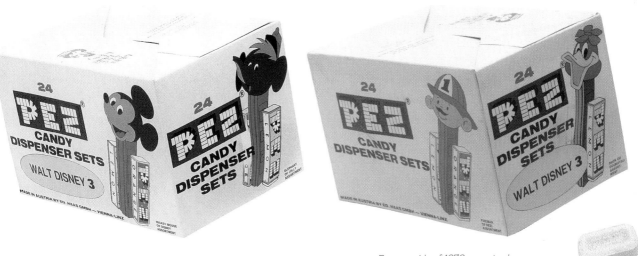

Outer cover of a 1970s counter box: $100+.

Reverse side of 1970s counter box.

Late 1970s
Superheroes box:
$200+.

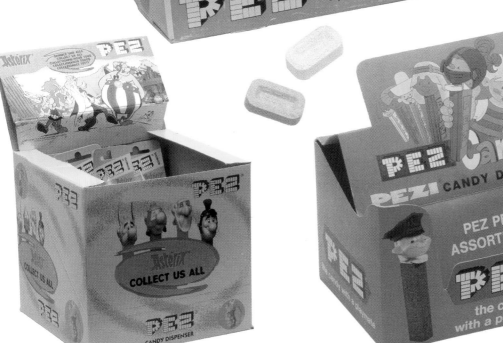

European Asterix box from the 1990s: $10-$20.

1970s PEZ® Pal box: $100+.

151

1970s Circus PEZ® box: $100+.

1970s Disney box: $150+.

A rare Jungle Book box from the 1960s: $400+.

Japanese candy refill boxes from the 1990s: $3-$5 each.

Japanese Peppermint refill box from the 1990s: $3-$5.

CHAPTER 20

Displays

1990s cardboard floor shippers. Some stores will let you have the empty display making a great way to display or store your extra dispensers.

Peter PEZ® spinner rack from the late 1980s early 1990s. $200-$250.

Display items include wire racks, cardboard floor boxes, plastic tabletop displays, and vending machines. PEZ® has relied little on advertising through the years and instead has concentrated on in-store impulse buying – aided greatly by eye-catching displays.

Store displays often feature various PEZ® characters and attractive artwork. Wire display racks often had cardboard header cards that could be changed to show different characters or promotions. Some collectors may choose to only collect these header signs as display racks can take up a lot of room.

In the late 1960s and early 1970s PEZ® was available in vending machines designed specifically for the dispensers. The dispensers were packaged in cardboard boxes that had the character's name printed on them. Even these boxes are considered quite collectible today.

1970s cardboard Peter PEZ® head for the top of a spinner rack. $85-$100.

Plastic Peter PEZ® head. This was the top of a spinner rack display in the 1970s. $100-$150.

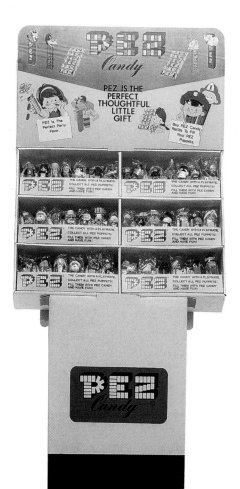

1970s cardboard floor display. $150-$200.

1960s Bloomfield mfg. vending machine. A little over 4' tall, this thing weighs a ton! Great display piece, very desirable among collectors. In good to excellent condition: $1500+.

Ad sheet for vending machine. $75+.

Metal vending machine sign from the 1960s measures 12"x19." $200+.

European vending machine, these are gaining popularity among collectors. The trend seems to favor original machines over restored models. Original $300-$500.

European wall mounted vending machine. Most of these are about 30 inches high and 10 inches wide, this particular model has been restored. Restored $250-$350.

(From the Johann Patek collection)

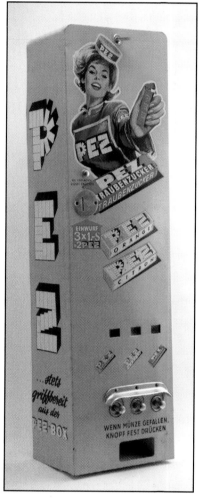

European vending machine. These date from
the late 1950s through the late 1970s. To
best determine age, you need to look at the
style of artwork and kind of candy
advertised on the outside of the machine.
(From the Johann Patek collection)

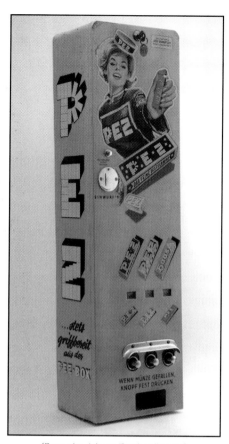

(From the Johann Patek collection)

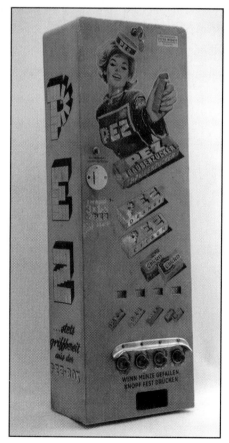

(From the Johann Patek collection)

(From the Johann Patek collection)

*(From the
Johann Patek
collection)*

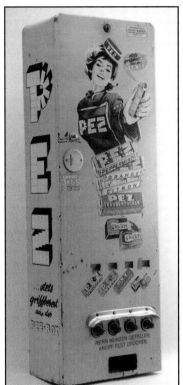

*(From the
Johann Patek
collection)*

Current wire display rack.

Small 1970s wire rack. $150-$200.

*1980s wire end-cap rack with metal PEZ®
header sign. (Note: this was made to hang from
existing store fixtures, the stand it is attached
to is for photo purposes.) $100-$150.*

D
I
S
P
L
A
Y
S

1970s vending machine boxes. (They will be worth more if the dispenser is still sealed inside the box.) $25-$35 each.

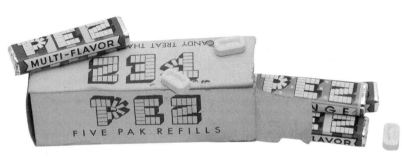

5 pack vending machine refill. $30-$40.

6 pack vending machine refill. $30-$40.

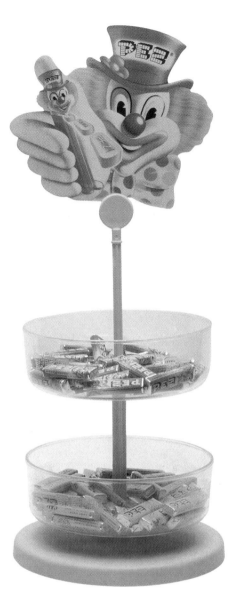

Tabletop Peter PEZ® display with acrylic bowls. From the 1990s, stands approximately 22" tall. $75-$100.

Various vending machine boxes from the 1960s (some boxes will be worth a little more depending on the character or artwork). $30-$40.

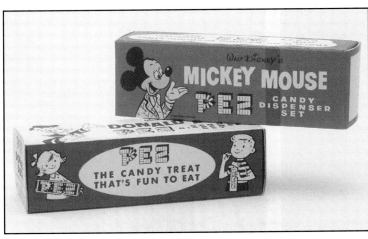

Unopened Mickey Mouse and Donald Duck vending machine boxes from the late 1960s/early 1970s. $50-$75 each.

Metal candy pack refill carousel from the 1950s. This one is missing the loop and header card that attaches to the top of the display. Can also be found in a red and yellow alternating panel version. Without the loop and header: $200-$250. Complete: $350-$400.

Smoke Pause display from the late 1950s made by Haas. It was sold as a breath mint for people between smokes. Individual candy packs: $15-$20. Display: $150+. (From the Maryann Kennedy collection)

1950s cardboard window display. The lady's arm folds out to create a 3-D effect as if she were handing you a Pez. A very rare item. $500+. (From the Maryann Kennedy collection)

D
I
S
P
L
A
Y
S

A very rare store display from the 1950s. She stands about 4 feet tall. $500+. (From the Silvia Biermayr/Gerhard Trebbin collection)

Christmas, PEZ® Pal, and Kooky Zoo header cards from the 1970s. $75-$100.

Bicentennial, Circus, and Mr. Ugly header cards from the 1970s. $75-$100.

European coin tray made of a melamine-like material, measures approximately 7" square. It was placed on the counter near the cash register and used to return customers' change. $20-$30.

PEZ® Western header card from Europe. This is what PEZ® sold in Europe in the mid-1970s in place of our Bicentennial series. Paperwork on this refers to the Indian Chief as "Winnetou", the Indian squaw as "Winnetou's schwester" (his sister), and the cowboy as "Old Shatterhand." $150+. (From the Maryann Kennedy collection)

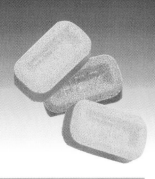

CHAPTER 21

Miscellaneous

PEZ® has never relied heavily on advertising so ad-related items are relatively scarce. More advertising items exist from Europe than from the U.S.

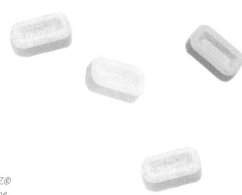

Metal sign showing PEZ® lady from the 1950s. Approx. 20" x 30" $200+. (From the Johann Patek collection)

Cardboard sign showing PEZ® lady, late 50s. $300+. (From the Johann Patek collection)

A rare European trolley or train advertising sign from the 1950s. Measures approximately 13"-17": $500+.

European theater programs from the 1940s and 1950s with PEZ® advertisement. Notice the one on the left, they used candy pack stickers like this to seal the program. One side of the sticker was stuck to the front and the other to the back. You had to break the seal in order to look at your program. Also pictured candy tin sold from 1934-1950: $200+, and unusual French PEZ® premium key chain: $30-$40.

1970s poster showing the PEZ® girl and Disney characters. Measures 24" x 33" $100-$150.

Comic ad from the 1980s and paper visors from the 1970s. Ad: $3-$5. Visors: $15-$20.

1970s PEZ® paper sack from Europe. $25-$30.

White Castle kids meal sack from 1990. The sack reads: "One Halloween Pez candy dispenser with every Castle Meal." $20-$25.

Body Parts

PEZ® introduced "Body Parts" in the mid-1990s. As the package states, "Body Parts are amusing attachable parts, with which you can dress up your PEZ® dispensers." The pieces snap on around the stem of the dispenser. The arms are movable and the hands are designed to hold various items.

First series of Body Parts. Left to right: red dress, nurse, purple dress, hockey player, skeleton, Robin Hood, Knight, and Tarzan. $1-$3.

M
I
S
C
E
L
L
A
N
E
O
U
S

Second series of Body Parts. Left to right: convict, cowgirl, legionnaire, caveman, roman soldier, and space robot. $1-$3.

Dispensers with body parts.

PEZ® Girls

In Europe the "PEZ® Girl" was used on advertising into the 1970s.

Old photo of the "PEZ® Girls."
(From the Silvia Biermayr/
Gerhard Trebbin collection)

An old photo showing the PEZ® lady handing out candy samples at an outdoor event. This photo was taken in Europe sometime in the early 1950s.

Tin European "postcards" with vintage artwork are from the 1990s and measure approximately 4"x6": $15-$20 each; European phone card holders from the 1990s: $2-$4 each; and PEZ® phone card (bottom center): $30-$40.

M
I
S
C
E
L
L
A
N
E
O
U
S

Gerda Jahn, one of the original models used to promote PEZ® candy! As a teenager she remembers entering a contest sponsored by PEZ® to become a model for the candy company. A kid's magazine called Bravo was used to promote the contest, and Gerda, along with 2 or 3 other girls won the contest. She was given a costume to wear and photos were taken of her in the classic PEZ® girl outfit. Gerhard Brause, a famous Austrian painter, used the photos to create a likeness of the girls. The images created by Brause were used on such things as vending machines, posters, and magazine advertisements. Although Gerda managed to land a few other modeling jobs not related to PEZ®, she continued to work at a hair salon and says she never promoted PEZ® at trade shows or conventions. She claims to still own the outfit she wore for the contest photos and says she never really collected the dispensers. Gerda now owns her own hair salon in Vienna and golf is her hobby of choice.

Gerda Jahn and author in Vienna, Austria, in May 2002.

1958 world expo in Brussels, Belgium. This photo was taken in Heysel Park and shows the PEZ® pavillion with some non-traditional looking PEZ® ladies handing out samples. The large structure in the background is called the "Atomium". It's the only remaining structure from the expo.

Different stylings of the PEZ® girl. Each of these photos is from the mid to late 1950s.

167

Premium Offers and Inserts

PEZ® has offered many premiums throughout the years and the premium insert sheets have become as collectible as the premiums themselves.

General Mills PEZ® premium offers from 2001. Specially marked boxes offered miniature dispensers of the Trix rabbit, Lucky Charms leprechaun, Honey Nut Cheerios bee, and Cocoa Puffs bird. Great graphics! Boxes with premiums $5-$8 each.

1984 Ralston Donkey Kong Jr. cereal box (front). This box advertises a mail-in offer for the Donkey Kong Jr. dispenser (monkey sailor with small "J" sticker on his cap). For 75 cents and 1 proof of purchase you got 1 Donkey Kong dispenser and 3 rolls of candy. Original box $200+ Reproduction box $20-$40.

Old European paper from the 1950s and '60s. These were used to store empty candy wrappers, and each folder contained squares to glue the wrapper. When full, you could redeem for the special premium offered. Advertisements showing the dispensers as full body characters are very desirable among collectors. $40-$75 each.

Back of box.

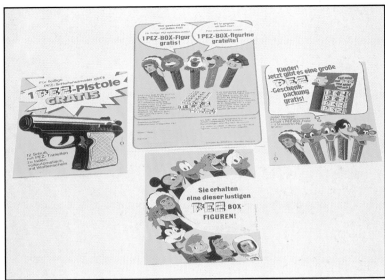

Snow White and several Maharajahs on a pentagon base. The base is marked "Pez" and was a mail-in premium in the 1960s. Found in a couple of different colors, ivory, as shown, is the most common. It holds 6 dispensers. $150-$200

German premium offers from the 1970s. The backside has individual spaces to glue candy wrappers. When it got full you mailed it in and received the current premium in return. $5-$10.

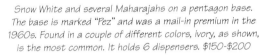

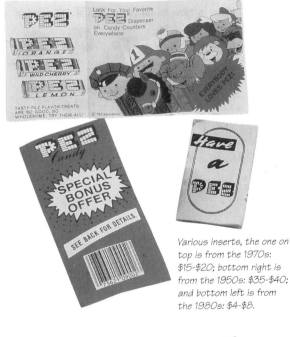

Rare 1950s space gun insert. The inside reads: "Dear Friend, COCOA MARSH is delighted to send you your free Pez space gun. Thank you for your continued loyalty to COCOA MARSH. We hope we can always live up to your families trust in us. With this in mind, we believe we have made COCOA MARSH with the finest chocolate syrup you can buy—the only leading chocolate syrup which contains vitamins B1, B2, D, and Iron. We hope, too, that you've had fun with our soda fountain pump. The best of health and happiness to you. Cordially, the Taylor-Reed Company, makers of COCOA MARSH." $65-$85.

Various inserts, the one on top is from the 1970s: $15-$20; bottom right is from the 1950s: $35-$40; and bottom left is from the 1980s: $4-$8.

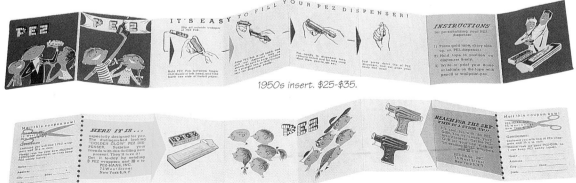

1950s insert. $25-$35.

Reverse side of 1950s insert.

Very hard to find comic ad from the 1970s featuring the rare Admiral. (Notice the pentagon stand offer is called "trophy pencil holder" and shows the Admiral dispenser in the back). $75+.
(From the Silvia Biermayer/ Gerhard Trebbin collection)

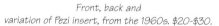

Front, back and variation of Pezi insert, from the 1960s. $20-$30.

Secret code flasher, Golden Glow, and T-shirt premium offer inserts. $15-$25.

Front and back, how to load your dispenser insert. $10-$20.

Golden glow and candy shooter offers: $15-$25; inserts with characters: $25-$35.

Inside of European PEZ® booklet. Measures approximately 4"x16." From the late 1950s or early 1960s: $40-$50.

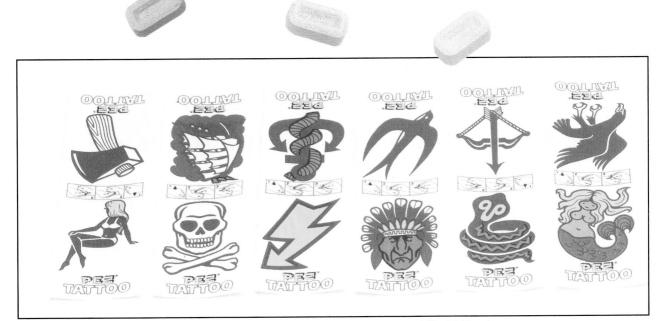

Tattoos! Offered as a premium with the dispenser in the 1970s. $3-$5 each.

Prototypes

Prototypes are also known as mock-ups. They are made of plaster and are representations of dispenser heads before the dispenser is actually produced. Collectors may sometimes find prototypes for heads that were never produced.

Everybody's favorite hamburger guy, Ronald McDonald. This rare plaster prototype is one of only two known to exist. PEZ® created it for McDonalds with the idea of making a Ronald McDonald PEZ® dispenser for the Happy Meal. The idea was scrapped after it was realized the enormous quantity needed would completely shut down PEZ® production to the point that they could make nothing but the one dispenser. (From the Maryann Kennedy collection)

Wow! Original polished steel dies for Santa 'A', Lions Club, and stem logos. It took one man three weeks to make just one section of the mold. (From the Johann Patek collection)

Plaster mock-ups (l. to r) Indian Whistle, Parrot Mmm, Penguin Mmm, Gargamel, Olympic Wolfs, and Easter Bunny. (From the Johann Patek collection)

Plaster mock-ups, very rare. Left to right: Three-piece Witch, Skull, Mr. Ugly, One-Eye Monster, Octopus, and Creature. (From the Dora Dwyer collection)

Panther, Betsy Ross, and Giraffe. These mock-ups are done on larger scale and are about the size of a billiard ball. (Fom the Johann Patek collection)

Truck and Indian Maiden. These are also large scale, the truck is approx. 6" long. (From the Johann Patek collection)

Mock-ups: PEZ® Pal, Lion with crown, and Make-a-Face. These are also done on large scale, each head is about the size of a baseball. From a tool-making standpoint, the Make-a-Face was a very difficult head to create. (From the Johann Patek collection)

173

Puzzles

German frame tray puzzle from the 1970s. $25-$35.

Ceaco brand puzzle. This appeared for a very brief time in the early 1990s. It was pulled from market because the makers did not secure proper rights to use the licensed characters. 125-piece puzzle: $40-$50. There is also a 550-piece version: $50-$70.

Hallmark "Pezzazle" puzzle from the mid-1990s. $15-$20.

Stickers and Clickers

Stickers were included in many of the dispenser and refill packages in the 1970s.

Round sticker doubles from the 1970s. These were free inside cellophane 6-pack candy refill packages. $5-$8 each.

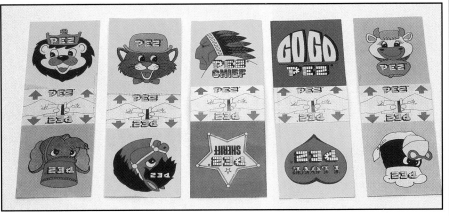

Square sticker doubles from the 1970s. These were also free inside candy refill packages. $3-$6 each.

Round sticker singles from the 1970s. These were a free premium offered inside some bagged dispensers. $5-$8 each.

Various clickers. $10-$20 each.

Unusual Packaging and Variations

Many packaging variations have been produced through the years. This is by no means a complete offering but a sample of some of the more unusual variations.

Crystal Snowman on Japanese "face candy" card and Crystal Icee Bear on floating candy card.

The Captain with a Bicentennial header card. Header card alone: $20-$40.

Trio of bagged dispensers with photo header card. (From the Johann Patek collection)

Reverse side of Spanish-made dispenser.

A Spanish-made dispenser mint in the bag. If you look closely you can see the country of origin on the stem is Spain. Dispensers marked Spain are very difficult to find. As pictured, $150-$200.

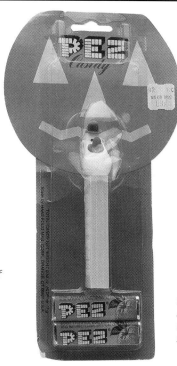

Clown with chin on a rare die-cut Halloween card. $200-$250.

176

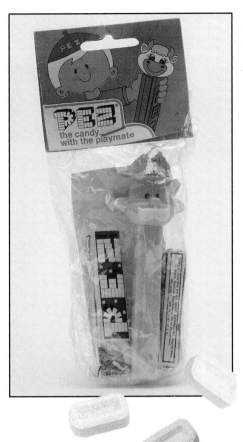

Fireman still in the bag
(notice the white
moustache, very unusu-
al). $150-$200.
(From the Maryann
Kennedy collection)

Back side of
the Fireman.

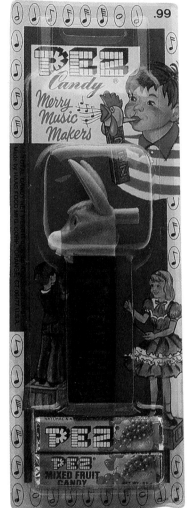

Donkey whistle still on original
card. $100-$125.

Unusual "PEZ® Rallye" card. $150-$200.

Unusual Chinese packaging. $40-$50.

M
I
S
C
E
L
L
A
N
E
O
U
S

Unique twin pack of glowing ghosts and a dinosaur gift pack, both only
released in Europe. $10-$15 each.

2+12 Box sets (non-U.S.). The 2 meant you got 2 dispensers and the
12 meant 12 packs of candy. $5-$10.

Gyro Gearloose on Japanese bubblepack. The one on the left is
the older version and the one on the right is the new updated
version.

Odds and Ends

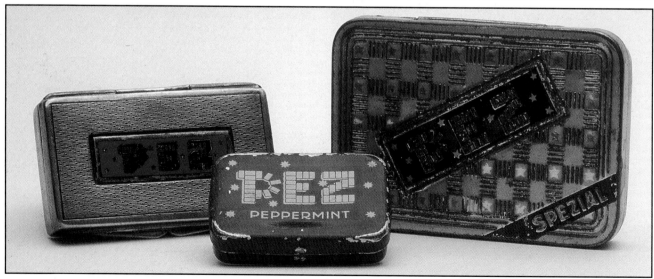

Original PEZ® tins. Before there was such thing as a PEZ® dispenser the candy was sold in tins like this. Very tough to find. The one on the left is from
the early 1930s: $200+. The small blue one in the middle dates to 1927: $200+. The one on the far right was sold from 1934 to 1950: $200+. There is
one other small round tin known with a picture of a car on top. It was called the "autobox": $200+. (From the Maryann Kennedy collection)

Candy tin from the Czech Republic. Measuring approximately 10" long, 7" wide, and 4" tall, it held 8 boxes of single pack refills. It is from the mid to late 1990s and is considered quite scarce. $75-$100.

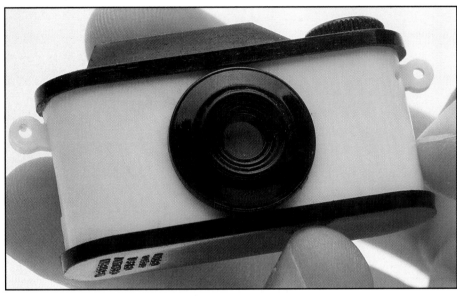

A very rare PEZ® item, less than five are known to exist. Called a "magic viewer," by holding it up to the light and looking through the back, you could see color pictures of Canada's championship hockey team. Pull the lever on the side and another picture would rotate through. The last slide shows a black and white picture of the PEZ® girl outside with skyscrapers in the background holding a regular. From the 1950s. $1000+. (From the Maryann Kennedy collection)

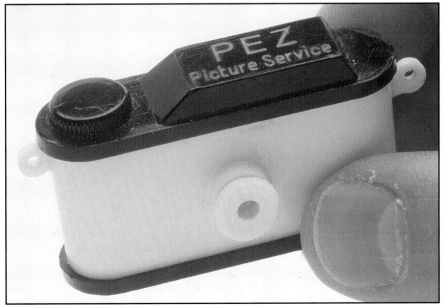

Back of PEZ® viewer.

This is an ink blotter from France. It was common for companies to print their advertisement on these and give them away. This one dates to the 1950s and is quite rare. It measures approximately 4"-6." $200+.

H.O. scale cars. $8-$12 each.

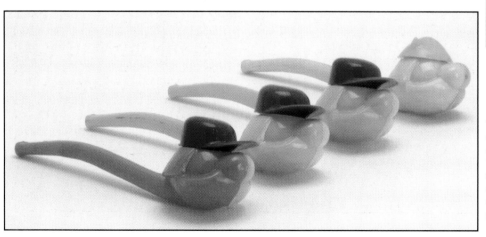

Bottom detail of H.O. scale car.

"TSCHIBUK" pipes translated, "old smoker." Pop the hat off, fill with PEZ® sherbet powder and water and enjoy! These are from the '70s and sell in the $65 range but can more than double in price for a rare version such as the horned hat character on the end. (From the Johann Patek collection)

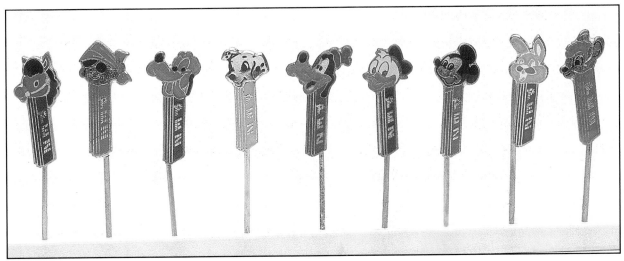

Lapel pins from the 1960s. $10-$15 each.

Various paper flags. $10-$15 each.

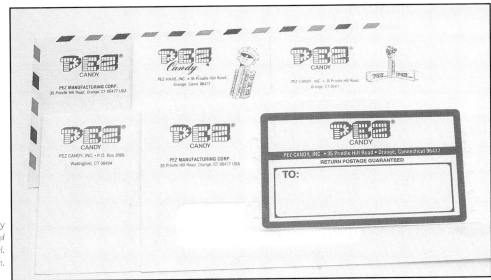

Company envelopes and shipping label. $3-$5 each.

CHAPTER 22

Conventions

Do you want to meet other collectors? Have lots of fun? See more PEZ® than you ever imagined? Attend a PEZ® convention! Conventions are one of the best ways to gain information and knowledge of the hobby, as well as to buy and sell PEZ®. You will find many rare and unusual items displayed, as well as organized events such as "Pez Bingo" to keep you busy.

Conventions have been sprouting up since the early 1990s, drawing people from all over the U.S and the world. Below you will find a current list of conventions, check *PEZ Collectors News* for exact times and dates.

1. Southern California – Conventions have been held since 1994 in several different locations with different hosts. Usually meets sometime in the spring.

2. St. Louis, Missouri – First convention held in 1993 and still going strong. Meets in June. Your host is John "CoolPezman" Devlin, who may be reached using the Web site, http://www.pezconvention.com or the 24-hour hotline: (314) 416-0333.

3. Bloomington, Minnesota – First convention held in October 1996 across from the Mall of America. Now meets in August rather than October. Your hosts are Dana and Julie Kraft, they may be reached using the Web site, www.MNPEZCON.com

4. Cleveland, Ohio – First ever PEZ® convention, "Dispensor-O-Rama" held June, 1991 in Mentor, Ohio. Continues to meet each July in the Cleveland area. Your host is Jill Cohen and she may be reached using the Web site, www.pezamania.com

5. Connecticut – Called the "East Coast PEZ® Convention" first met in April 1999 in Orange, Connecticut (home of PEZ® Candy, Inc.). Moved to a larger location in Stamford, CT for the May 2000 show. Your host is Richie Belyski (editor of *PEZ Collectors News*) and he may be reached using the Web site, www.pezcollectorsnews.com or at the following address:

PEZ Collector's News
P.O. Box 14956
Surfside Beach, SC 29587

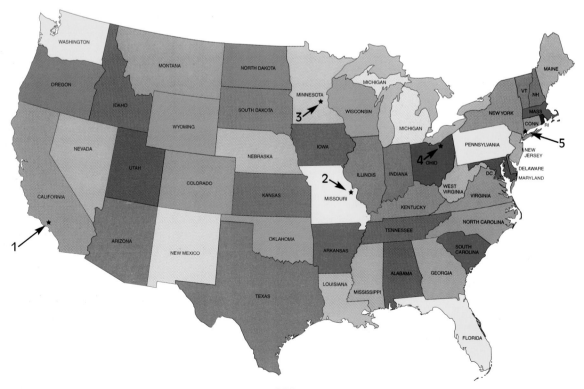

CHAPTER 23

Finding Information

Several newsletters have been dedicated to collecting PEZ®. The first, *The Toy Candy Container and Food Premium Collector*, appeared in 1987. With the third issue the name changed to *The Old Variety Store*. The *OVS* lasted until late 1989 and had a run of about 15 issues. In January 1990, the *Optimistic Pezzimist* came on board. It too had a run of just 15 issues, lasting until July of 1992. Without much delay, in the fall of 1992 the *Positively Pez* newsletter was started.

By this time the hobby was gaining steam. The first book about PEZ® had been released during the previous year, and collectors were becoming more knowledgeable than ever. *Positively Pez* had a run of 19 issues and ended with the January/February 1996 edition. With the announcement of its close, and with an ever-growing number of collectors hungry for the latest PEZ® information, two new publications were started. The *Fliptop Pezervation Society* premiered with the September/October 1995 issue, billing itself as "the first national club for PEZ® collectors." Pedro PEZ®, a boy PEZ® Pal dispenser, was adopted as the club mascot and was sent around the world with various collectors visiting interesting places and having his picture taken.

Right on the heels of the *Fliptop* newsletter, *PEZ Collectors News* made its first appearance with the October/November 1995 issue. The two newsletters worked well together, uniting collectors and giving them more information than ever before. In December 1999, the *Fliptop Pezervation Society* announced that the September/October 1999 issue was their last and they would combine efforts with *PEZ Collectors News*. *FPS* enjoyed a run of 24 issues. Currently *PEZ Collectors News*, put out bimonthly by Richie Belyski, is the only newsletter devoted to PEZ®. You can contact them at:

PEZ Collector's News
P.O. Box 14956
Surfside Beach, SC 29587
E-mail: info@pezcollectorsnews.com
http://www.pezcollectorsnews.com

PEZ® IN SPACE

PEZ® in Space? Cyberspace, that is. A ton of information about PEZ® can be found on the Internet. It is an excellent source for up-to-date information and a great way to buy and sell PEZ®. There are hundreds, maybe even thousands, of sites built by collectors that detail everything from how to properly load your dispenser to pictures of personal collections.

One of the nicest collector-built sites is Pez Central. Good design, great graphics and pictures, up-to-date information, and links to other Web pages make it a great place to visit. Check it out at: www.pezcentral.com.

Another great online source to gather information, meet other collectors and find out what's happening in the PEZ collecting world is the PEZHEAD LIST! Membership is free, but you will need to register first. Find it by going to: http://groups.yahoo.com/group/PEZheads.

By now there are probably very few people who haven't heard of eBay. But did you know that eBay got its start with PEZ®? Pierre Omidyar, founder of eBay, originally created the site as a way for his girlfriend to buy and sell PEZ® dispensers. To accomplish this, Omidyar built an Internet auction site that brought buyer and seller together on a level playing field. In doing so he created one of the most popular and fastest growing places on the Internet. There are now three PEZ® categories—General, Current, and Vintage—which offer an average of more than 3,000 items a week. You can find the site at: www.ebay.com.

PEZ® Candy, Inc. also has a Web site. Within their site you will find a FAQ list (Frequently Asked Questions), a list of PEZ® Dispensers offered to date in the United States, a list of other cool PEZ® products, information about PEZ® newsletters, and the PEZ® Store. The store sells many current dispensers and candy flavors, including some items that are unique and only available through the special mail-order program. The site can be found at: www.pez.com.

STARTING UP

If you are a new collector you are probably wondering how to get started. Start out slowly—look for all of the current release dispensers you can find around your town. That alone will give you a nice size collection on which to build without spending too much money. Most collectors ask the questions: "Should I leave it in the package or open it up?" and "Will it loose its value if I open it?" Opening the dispenser is a matter of preference. If the dispenser is old, I would advise against opening the package. With the new stuff, it's up to you. Personally, I buy at least three of each new release; one in the bag, one on the card to save, and one to open for display. It's true, a carded or bagged dispenser is traditionally worth more than one that is loose, but a dispenser out of package is more fun to display.

Next, move on to the current European dispensers. Most of these can be had for $3 to $4 each. Acquire all of these and the size of your collection will almost double. When it comes to vintage dispensers, decide what your first "price plateau" will be and start from there. For example, there are still a good number of footless dispensers that can be found for $35 or less. Once you buy all of these, move on to the next price level and so on.

Although some of the old dispensers reach into the hundreds and even thousands of dollars, you don't have to spend your life savings to enjoy the hobby. Some collectors specialize and focus on collecting one favorite area such as the Animals or PEZ® Pal series. Others focus on stems by collecting a character that is made in several different countries, or by collecting as many different colors as they can. A good example of this is the Teenage Mutant Ninja Turtles. There are

Droopy dispenser only available in Europe. The card on the left is the older style striped card; on the right is an updated card that resembles the American card.

eight different dispensers that come on eight different stem colors, if you were to collect all of the combinations you would have 64 turtles alone in your collection!

The most important thing to remember about collecting PEZ®... it's a hobby—have fun!

BUTTON- an opaque rectangle piece inside the stem, usually red but sometimes white, that the candy actually sits on. There are a couple versions: a rectangle with square corners, and a rectangle with rounded corners. The square corner version is the oldest.

CHANNEL- the groove on the front of the dispenser that runs the length of the stem.

CLUB MED- a term used when a character's face appears very tan, as if they have been in the sun or at Club Med. This can also be considered a color variation.

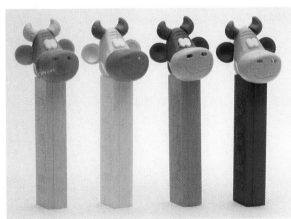

COLOR VARIATION- refers to the comparison of like dispensers in which one has a different color to the entire head or to one or more of the parts found on the head. Example:a cow may have a head that is yellow, blue, orange, green etc. The possibilities are almost infinite.

DBP- the German patent number on a dispenser. It means 'Deutsches Bundes Patent' and will be accompanied by the numbers 818 829

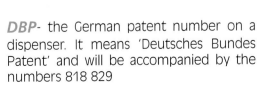

Thin foot version on the left, thicker current version on the right.

This is one of only a few examples of an early footed dispenser known to exist.
(From the Maryann Kennedy collection)

FEET- small rounded plastic protrusions or tabs at the base of the stem to help the dispenser stand upright. Feet were added to dispensers in the U.S. around 1987. Currently there are 2 different styles. The earlier version is known as 'thin feet', referring to the fact that the plastic of the feet is not as thick as the plastic feet found on current dispensers. Beware, some people try to cut the feet off and pass them off as a footless dispenser. Some dispensers were produced both ways, with feet and without. Look to the spine of the stem to tell if it has been altered.

HEAD- The top most part of the dispenser that tilts back to dispense the candy.

IMC- Injection Mold Code. A single digit number found on the outside top corner of the stem. Identifies in which plastic factory the dispenser was molded. Not all dispensers have IMC's. Here is a list to help identify which number goes with which country:

1 & 3- Austria/ Hungary
2- Austria/ Hong Kong
4 & 8 - Austria
5- Yugoslavia/ Slovenia
6- Hong Kong/ China
7- Hong Kong/ Austria/ Czech Republic
9- U.S.A.
V- Yugoslavia (changed to Slovenia in 1993)

KICKER- Sometimes referred to as the "pusher", this is the small plastic piece that extends down from the back of the head and pushes out a single piece of candy when the head is tilted back.

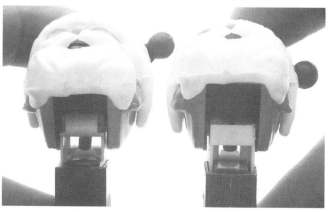

Blade type spring on the left and "classic wire" mechanism on the right.
The kicker is shown just below the spring.

LOOSE- the dispenser is out of its original packaging.

MARBELIZED- a term used when two or more colors of plastic are combined and not thoroughly mixed, causing a swirling pattern to appear in the finished product. This is a sought after variation by some collectors.

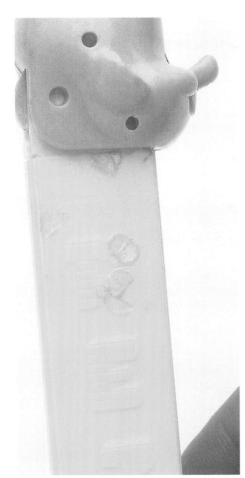

MELT MARK- refers to damage on the dispenser. Sometimes caused by direct heat or a chemical reaction between the plastic of the dispenser and certain types of rubber or other plastics. Certain types of rubber bands and items like rubber-fishing worms have been known to cause melt marks when left in contact with a dispenser.

M.I.B.- Mint In Bag. Bag will have colored ends and writing as well as the PEZ® logo. Newer style. Also known as a 'poly bag.'

M.I.C.- Mint In Cellophane or Mint In Cello. Bag will be clear with no writing.

M.O.C.- Mint On Card

M.O.M.C.- Mint On Mint Card. Both dispenser and card are in pristine condition.

N/F- no feet

PATENT NUMBER- seven digit number located on the side of the stem. Currently there are six different U.S. patent numbers on PEZ® dispensers: 2, 620, 061 is the earliest, followed by 3,410,455; 3,845,882; 3,942, 683; 4,966,305; and 5,984,285. 3,370,746 was issued for the candy shooter and appears on the 1980s space gun as well. Patent numbers can help identify the age of a dispenser but generally do not play a part in its value. Not all dispensers have a patent number on them, certain dispensers have no patent numbers, this does not affect the value of those dispensers. Feet first started to appear on dispenser bases when the 3,942,683 number was issued but some exceptions can be found with feet and earlier issue patent numbers. These dispensers are difficult to find and carry a little more value with some collectors.

2.6 patent close up with thin feet. This is a rare oddity.

An example of the unusual patent marking usually found only on the holiday witch.

PEZHEAD- a term used to describe someone who collects PEZ®!

PIN- steel pin that hinges the head. Made of metal and found only in older dispensers. The 'pin' runs through the side of the head and the sleeve, attaching it to the dispenser base.

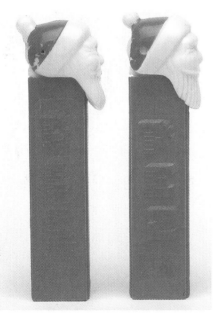

Metal pin on left, plastic hinge pins on right.

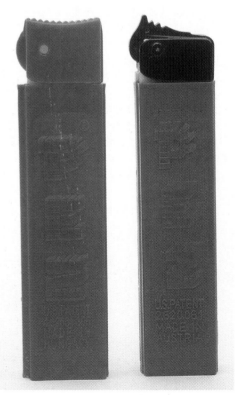

Remake on the left, vintage on the right.

REGULAR- The earliest PEZ® dispensers. These didn't have a character head; instead they had only a thumb grip at the top and were marketed for adults. These were remade in the late 1990s but with a noticeable difference. Vintage regulars will have a raised thumb grip on the top of the cap. The remakes will have a square cap with no raised grip and the spine will be deeper than the channel.

Original shoe shown on far left.

SHOES- An accessory for your dispenser that fits on the base of the stem. Similar to feet in that its purpose is to give the dispenser more stability when standing upright. Originally made to be used with the Make-a-Face dispenser. Reproduction shoes have been made with a rounded toe in the front, and can be found in at least three colors: black, white, and red. There is also a reproduction glow-in-the-dark version. An original shoe will always be black and have a 'B' shape to the end.

SLEEVE- the part of the dispenser that pulls out of the stem and holds the candy. The United States patent description refers to this part as the magazine.

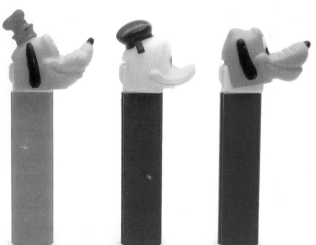

SOFT-HEAD- the head is made of a rubber, eraser-like material that is pliable and softer than traditional plastic head dispensers, hence the name 'soft-head'. Soft -heads can be found in the Eerie Specter and Super Hero series, along with a very rare Disney set that never made it to mass production.

Vintage footless dispenser on left;
footed dispenser with feet removed on right.

SPINE- the groove on the back of the dispenser that runs the length of the stem. On a vintage footless dispenser the spine should be the same depth as the channel. Some unscrupulous people will try to pass off a dispenser as footless by cutting off the feet and claiming that it is old. To detect tampering, turn the dispenser upside down and compare the spine to the channel. The spine on a footed dispenser will always be deeper than its channel.

SPRING- refers to either the spring inside the stem directly under the button, OR the spring in the top of the dispenser that keeps tension on the character head. There are 3 basic types of springs in the top of the dispenser: the classic wire mechanism, the blade spring, and currently a 'leaf spring' mechanism.

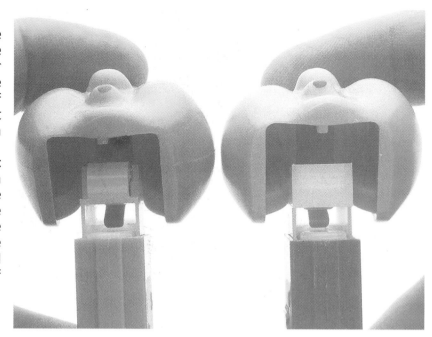

Blade spring on the left, current "leaf spring" on the right.

STEM- the lower part of the dispenser. Usually has the PEZ® logo on at least one side and possibly country of origin, patent number, and injection mold code. Depending on the dispenser, the stem may also be die-cut or be completely smooth on one or both sides.

TRANSITION PIECE- a dispenser that has characteristics of a previous model but also has features of a current dispenser. These pieces must still be in their original packaging to show they are void of alterations. Example: an old style character head that is on a footed stem.

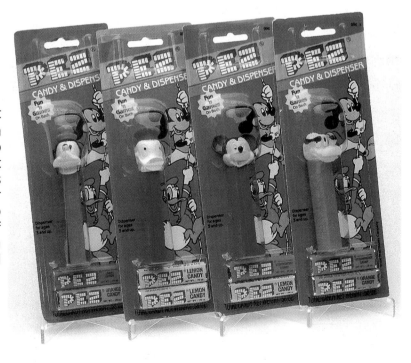

W/F- with feet.

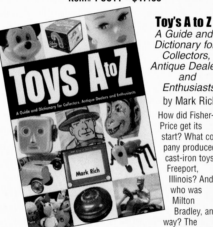
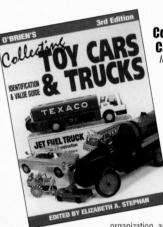